The Sixth 200
Questions Answered
By Dr. D. A. Waite

?

Real Questions From Real
People With Real Answers

Published by

THE BIBLE FOR TODAY PRESS
900 Park Avenue
Collingswood, New Jersey 08108
U.S.A.
Pastor D. A. Waite, Th.D., Ph.D.
𝕭𝖎𝖇𝖑𝖊 𝕱𝖔𝖗 𝕿𝖔𝖉𝖆𝖞 𝕭𝖆𝖕𝖙𝖎𝖘𝖙 𝕮𝖍𝖚𝖗𝖈𝖍
Church Phone: 856-854-4747
BFT Phone: 856-854-4452
Orders: 1-800-John 10:9
e-mail: BFT@BibleForToday.org
Website: www.BibleForToday.org
Fax: 856-854-2464

We Use and Defend
The King James Bible

August, 2013
BFT 4058

ISBN #978-1-56848-087-9

Acknowledgments

I wish to acknowledge the assistance of the following people:

- **Yvonne Sanborn Waite**--my wife, for encouraging me to publish these questions and answers, for reading the manuscript carefully; for putting in various boxes; and for giving other helpful suggestions for the body of the book and the cover.
- **Anne Marie Noyle**–a faithful supporter of our **Bible For Today** ministries and an attender via the Internet of our **Bible For Today Baptist Church**, who read the book several times and gave many valuable suggestions.

FOREWORD

- **Fourteen Chapters**. This is the 6th series of 200 questions that have been sent to me (## 1001-1200). I have answered them as simply and as clearly as possible. The answers to the 1st questions ##1-200 can be found in **BFT #3309** @ **$14.00 + $7.00 S&H**. The answers to the 2nd questions ##201-400 can be found in **BFT #3473** @ **$14.00 + $7.00 S&H**. The answers to the 3rd questions ##401-600 can be found in **BFT #3482** @ **$14.00 + $7.00 S&H**. The answers to the 4th questions ##601-800 can be found on **BFT #3494** @ **$14.00 + $7.00 S&H**. The answers to the 5th questions ##801-1000 can be found on **BFT #4014** @ **$14.00 + $7.00 S&H**.

- **Some Of The Question Topics**. In this 6th question and answer book (**BFT #4058** @ **$14.00 + $7.00 S&H**), there are questions about Theology and Doctrine; various People; the King James Bible; Bible Versions; Greek Manuscripts; the Behavior of Christians; the Chinese Union Version (CUV); the New Testament; Bible Inspiration; Dispensationalism, the Spanish Bible, Bible Preservation; and seven Miscellaneous Topics.

- **Various Questions and Answers Might Be Similar**. I have tried not to duplicate questions and answers in this sixth book. However, various things should be understood by the readers. Similar questions might have been asked in books one, two, three, four, or five. Similar questions might also have been asked in this sixth book. But if there is a slightly different emphasis either in the question, or in my answer, I have included them. Be sure to consult the very detailed INDEX in this book to help you.

D. A. Waite

Pastor D. A. Waite, Th.D., Ph.D.
Director of the **Bible For Today**, Incorporated, and
Pastor of the **Bible For Today Baptist Church**

Table of Contents

The Sixth 200 Questions Answered By Dr. D. A. Waite

?

Introductory Considerations

Have you received your copy of *THE FIRST 200 QUESTIONS ANSWERED* (**BFT #3909 @ $15.00 + $7.00 S&H**)? Have you received your copy of *THE SECOND 200 QUESTIONS ANSWERED* (**BFT #3473 @ $15.00 + $7.00 S&H**)? Have you received your copy of *THE THIRD 200 QUESTIONS ANSWERED* (**BFT #3482 @ $15.00 + $7.00 S&H**)? Have you received your copy of *THE FOURTH 200 QUESTIONS ANSWERED* (**BFT #3494 @ $15.00 + $7.00 S&P**). Have you received your copy of *THE FIFTH 200 QUESTIONS ANSWERED* (**BFT #4014 @ $15.00 + $7.00 S&P**). If not, you might want to get a copy of each of these books and read them along with the present book of *THE SIXTH 200 QUESTIONS ANSWERED* (**BFT #4058 @ $15.00 + $7.00 S&P**).

Though there might be some general topics here that were included in either the first, second, third, fourth, or fifth book, these are asked by different people at different times and in different ways. My answers are also different in various ways.

CHAPTER I
QUESTIONS ABOUT
THEOLOGY AND DOCTRINE

"Believe" Versus "Believing"

QUESTION #1001

Would you shed some understanding to me as to the word, *"believe,"* as translated by the King James Bible translators? Arminians contend that the Greek word for *"believe"* in John 3:16; 6:47; 18:6, and others, is in the present continuous tense and should read *"believing"* instead of *"believe."* What is the rebuttal to such claim? Could you point me in the right direction to obtain an answer? May I quote your answer if I should write a book refuting conditional security if I needed? Thank you very much in advance.

ANSWER #1001

What this man fails to understand is that there are many special uses of the Greek present tense, in addition to the regular uses which are progressive. There is the aoristic present which is a reference to past time, or punctiliar action in present time, not progressive action (Dana & Mantey's *Manual Grammar of the Greek New Testament*, page 184). Or it could be a historical present which is a past event viewed with the vividness of a present occurrence (p. 185). Or it could be a tendential present or a static present (p. 186).

This man who believes you can lose your salvation based on the Greek present tense in the passages he quotes simply is ignorant of the various uses of the Greek Present Tense. You can quote anything I have said to you or what is found in any of my books so long as credit is given for the quote. I think you are wasting your time trying to convince a man with these beliefs that he is wrong. He will not be convinced no matter what you write to him. I would suggest you just *"let him alone"* as the Lord Jesus Christ advised His disciples concerning the offended Pharisees in Matthew 15:12-14.

Matthew 15:12-14

*"Then came his disciples, and said unto him, Knowest thou that the **Pharisees were offended**, after they heard this saying? But he answered and said, Every plant, which my heavenly Father hath not planted, shall be*

*rooted up. **Let them alone: they be blind leaders of the blind. And if the blind lead the blind, both shall fall into the ditch**.*"

The Meaning of "Righteous"
QUESTION #1002

What is meant by "*the righteous*" in Matthew 9:13? Is it pertaining to the born-again believers who have become righteous through Jesus Christ?

ANSWER #1002

"*But go ye and learn what that meaneth, I will have mercy, and not sacrifice: for I am not come to call **the righteous**, but sinners to repentance.*" (Matthew 9:13)

The word, "*righteous*," (DIKAIOUS) occurs 37 times in the New Testament. As in the verse, I believe it sometimes means (depending on the context) "*those who only **think** they are righteous,*" but are not necessarily "*righteous*" in God's eyes. For example, in Matthew 28:28:

"*Even so ye also outwardly **appear righteous** unto men, but within ye are full of hypocrisy and iniquity.*"

Here again, this word (DIKAIOI) us used for phony righteousness, not true righteousness. In Luke 18:9:

"*And he spake this parable unto certain which trusted in themselves that they were **righteous**, and despised others:*"

These are phonies also.

> There is no other way to become truly and Biblically "*righteous*" except by being redeemed by genuinely trusting the Lord Jesus Christ for His salvation. It is certainly possible that this is what is meant here, regardless of other meanings elsewhere.

Judged "According to Works"
QUESTION #1003
Revelation 20:12

"*And I saw the dead, small and great, stand before God; and the books were opened: and another book was opened, which is the book of life: and the dead were **judged** out of those things which were written in the books, **according to their works**.*"

What does this verse mean? Surely we are not saved by works but by God's Grace. Why does it say "*judged . . . according to their works*"?

ANSWER #1003

This verse is describing what is called the great white throne judgment. It is a judgment of people who are lost and who have never genuinely trusted the Lord Jesus Christ as their Saviour. I believe all the people present before the Lord Jesus Christ, the Judge, will be cast into the lake of everlasting fire. However, I believe the Bible teaches that there will be degrees of punishment in that lake of fire which will be determined by the Lord Jesus Christ "*according to their works.*" This is seen in the following verses:

Matthew 11:22

"*But I say unto you, It shall be **more tolerable** for Tyre and Sidon at the day of judgment, than for you.*"

Mark 6:11

"*And whosoever shall not receive you, nor hear you, when ye depart thence, shake off the dust under your feet for a testimony against them. Verily I say unto you, It shall be **more tolerable** for Sodom and Gomorrha in the day of judgment, than for that city.*"

Sodom and Gomorrha will have a lesser punishment in Hell than the city who has rejected the testimony of the disciples of the Lord Jesus Christ.

> This matter of "*degrees*" of punishment for the lost is similar in principle to the various "*degrees*" of blessing for the saved in Heaven depending on what materials they build upon the Lord Jesus Christ, their "*Foundation,*" (1 Corinthians 3:11-15) whether "*wood, hay, stubble*" or "*gold, silver, precious stones.*" Reward will be given only for the use of the latter materials which have been built on the Lord Jesus Christ, the believer's "*Foundation.*"

New Testament Questions

QUESTION #1004

Why is there a difference between Matthew 8:5-13 which reads that it was the centurion who came to Jesus? In Luke 7:1-10, it was the servant who approached Jesus. How do we understand what happened?

Matthew 8:5

"*And when Jesus was entered into Capernaum, **there came unto him a centurion**, beseeching him,*"

Luke 7:2-3

"*And a certain centurion's servant, who was dear unto him, was sick, and ready to die. And when he heard of Jesus, **he sent unto him the elders of the Jews**, beseeching him that he would come and heal his servant.*"

ANSWER #1004

Though there seems to be a contradiction here, it could be two separate accounts spoken of by Matthew and Luke. In both cases, (1) there was a centurion; (2) There was a servant who was sick; and (3) The Lord Jesus Christ healed the centurion's servant.

Contentions About Men's Long Hair

QUESTION #1005

What do you believe Paul meant when he said:

1 Corinthians 11:16

"But if any man seem to be contentious, we have no such custom, neither the churches of God"?

He had been discussing the issue of men's and women's hair in this chapter of 1 Corinthians.

ANSWER #1005

It quite possibly could mean that neither Paul nor the *"churches of God"* had any *"custom"* of *"contentiousness."* That would fit in with verse 17:

"Now in this that I declare unto you I praise you not, that ye come together not for the better, but for the worse."

I do not believe that the clear teachings of verses 13, 14, and 15 for the men and the women can in any way be obliterated by v. 16 or any other verse. We had a long-haired man attend our services years ago who used verse 16 to justify it. I disagreed with him.

Believing and Eternal Life

QUESTION #1006

Acts 13:48

"And when the Gentiles heard this, they were glad, and glorified the word of the Lord: and as many as were ordained to eternal life believed."

In Acts 13:48, can the sentence *"as many as were ordained to eternal life believed."* be translated to *"as many as those believed were ordained eternal life for them"*? Does this violate Greek grammar?

ANSWER #1006

I think your suggested translation is possible. In the Greek language, the verb, *"believed,"* does come before the word, *"ordained."* In view of this, the translation could be as you suggest. This does not violate Greek grammar.

New Testament Questions

QUESTION #1007

Romans 6:6

"Knowing this, that <u>our old man</u> is crucified with him, that the body of sin might be destroyed, that henceforth <u>we should not serve sin</u>."

My question is what does Romans 6:6 mean?

ANSWER #1007

I believe it is God's will that every born-again Christian should *"not serve sin"* (the sin nature). Since saved people have two natures, only if he or she is "filled" or controlled by the Holy Spirit can he or she not *"serve"* the sin nature at any given moment. Saved people have been *"crucified with Christ"* (Galatians 2:20) in order to empower them. Galatians 5 clearly spells out the battle between a saved person's flesh and God the Holy Spirit Who indwells him. I believe that when a saved person is walking in the power of God the Holy Spirit who indwells him, he can be called *"spiritual"* at that moment of time. Likewise, when a saved person is manifesting any of the works of the flesh (outlined in Galatians 5), at that time, he can be called *"carnal."*

Has Christ Come In The Flesh?

QUESTION #1008

You profess to believe, preach, and/or teach the word of God. According to I John 4:1 there are many false prophets gone out into the world, so we are commanded by God to try the spirits. Therefore, you are being tried to see whether or not you are of God: Do you confess that Jesus Christ is come in the flesh according to I John 4:2?

I admonish you to do so immediately.

A non answer is a non confession.

What is your confession?

I will give you my confession as if you had asked me:

I confess that Jesus Christ is come in the flesh.

I John 4:1-3

"Beloved, believe not every spirit, but try the spirits whether they are of God: because many false prophets are gone out into the world. Hereby know ye the Spirit of God: Every spirit that confesseth that Jesus Christ is come in the flesh is of God: And every spirit that confesseth not that Jesus Christ is come in the flesh is not of God: and this is that spirit of antichrist, whereof ye

have heard that it should come; and even now already is
it in the world."

I await your swift reply. A non answer is a non confession.

ANSWER #1008

Yes. Of course I believe that the Lord Jesus Christ is come in the flesh without any question.

Prophetic Questions

QUESTION #1009

I was reading an article and in it it said that all the events described in Matthew 24 will take place at a time when the Gospel has been preached to all the world which hasn't happened yet. It also said that the Book of Revelation reveals that this will not be accomplished until late in the Tribulation when God will send forth an angel who will preach the "*everlasting gospel*" to "*every nation and tribe and tongue and people*" (Revelation 14:6). If this is so, then it would mean that Bible translations in every language would not necessarily have to be accomplished before the Tribulation Period--is this correct?

ANSWER #1009

This is correct. If Bible translations had to be completed in all languages before the Tribulation, the rapture of the saved could not be imminent–which it is. Nothing needs to be fulfilled before the any-minute rapture of the genuinely born-again Christians.

The Word, "Theology"

QUESTION #1010

Is the word, "*theology*," mentioned in the Bible?

ANSWER #1010

No, it is not. It means the "*study and teachings about God*." It is a useful and descriptive term.

The Lord Jesus Christ's Lineage

QUESTION #1011

I am slightly confused about the lineage of the Lord Jesus Christ and could use some authentic information about it. Matthew 1:1-16 traces the line of Joseph the legal father of Jesus Christ and basically points to His line of King David, thereby proving He is in the lineage of the Kings. Luke 3:23-38 seems to trace again Joseph back to Adam, son of God, proving that He is the 2nd Adam, and directly descended from God.

Where does Mary come lineage-wise? Mary was a cousin to Elizabeth who was of the daughters of Aaron of the tribe of Levi (Luke 1:5). So why do not the Gospels trace the lineage of Christ through the tribe of Levi? Some say that Mary's lineage is traced in Luke 3:23-38, but there is no mention of Mary. It ties Christ again to Judah son of Jacob and his Kingship. So, where have I gone wrong? I know that the book of Hebrews points out that Christ, as the High Priest, came through Melchisedec, totally outside of the lineage of Aaron and the tribe of Levi. So I could use your help.

ANSWER #1011

I believe that Mary's lineage is in Luke 3. Joseph's lineage is in Matthew 1. This lineage goes through David which is cursed because of Coniah or Jeconiah as in Jeremiah's account.

> Jeremiah 22:24   *"As I live, saith the LORD, though **Coniah the son of Jehoiakim** king of Judah were the signet upon my right hand, yet would I pluck thee thence;"*
> Jeremiah 22:28 *"Is this man **Coniah** a despised broken idol? is he a vessel wherein is no pleasure? wherefore are they cast out, he and his seed, and are cast into a land which they know not?*

The Lord Jesus Christ did not come from the tribe of Levi. He came from the tribe of Judah through the line of David. Melchisedec was an angel or a Christophany (Christ Himself in His pre-incarnate state). He was not a human being.

> Hebrews 7:3 *"Without father, without mother, without descent, having neither beginning of days, nor end of life; but **made like unto the Son of God**; abideth a priest continually."*

The Lord Jesus Christ's priesthood bypasses that of Levi and is superior to it as Melchisedec's priesthood was higher than that of Levi.

Doctrinal Questions

QUESTION #1012

I purchased one of your *Defined King James Bible* in August, 2009, and have been using it frequently. I noticed that in Titus 1:9 the word *"doctrine"* is bolded and defined as *"healthy"* but it should be the word *"sound"* which is defined as *"healthy."* Also, I would suggest a good concordance in the back of your Bible.

#1001–1200 Questions   By Dr. D. A. Waite

ANSWER #1012

You are correct. In Titus 1:9, "*sound*" should have been bolded. A sound and complete concordance would be too costly and bulky for our *Defined King James Bible*. The computer is the way to go for a concordance. I'll send your Titus 1:9 suggestion to our son, D. A. Waite, Jr., who wrote the notes.

Christ's Bodily Ascension
QUESTION #1013

I do want to ask you a Bible question. This is very serious! I maintain that shortly after Our Lord Jesus Christ was resurrected from the tomb, He ascended to Heaven, after talking to Mary Magdeline, to place His precious, innocent Blood on the Heavenly mercy seat. I believe that the Lord Jesus Christ is God. A friend of mine disagrees with me. She is in the Seventh Day Adventist church. She maintains that our Lord Jesus Christ never left earth for forty days after his resurrection. Can you give me your opinion?

ANSWER #1013

I concur with your opinion that the Lord Jesus Christ, the Great High Priest of the redeemed ones, just after His bodily resurrection, went to Heaven and put some of His perfect, precious, and sinless Blood on the Heavenly Mercy Seat. This is supported by the analogy of what the high priests in Israel did on the day of atonement (Leviticus 16), and by the clear teachings in the book of Hebrews.

False Teachers
QUESTION #1014

How often do you get responses with hostility when you try to show the truth even to your closest brethren about the King James Bible, false teachers, or other things?

ANSWER #1014

Hostility comes often to those of us who stick closely to Biblical truth among those who do not wish to stick so closely. Don't let it get you down. Be glad the Lord has given you insight into His Words. As the Lord Jesus Christ told His disciples about the Pharisees who were "*OFFENDED*": We should also "*LET THEM ALONE.*"

*"Then came his disciples, and said unto him, Knowest thou that **the Pharisees were offended**, after they heard this saying? But he answered and said, Every plant, which my heavenly Father hath not planted, shall be rooted up. **Let them alone: they be blind leaders of the blind**. And if the blind lead the blind, both shall fall into the ditch."* (See Matthew 15:12-14.)

Ezekiel 37 Fulfillment

QUESTION #1015

When will Ezekiel 37 be fulfilled?

ANSWER #1015

Ezekiel 37 will not be fulfilled until the millennial reign of the Lord Jesus Christ. At that time, both the ten tribes of Northern Israel and the two tribes of Southern Israel will come to the Lord Jesus Christ for salvation. Israel as a whole nation has not done this as yet. They have generally rejected the Lord Jesus Christ as their Messiah.

The Attributes of Christ on Earth

QUESTION #1016

Though the Lord Jesus Christ gave up the use of His Divine attributes for His own purposes, were those attributes still possessed by Him while He was on this earth?

ANSWER #1016

The Lord Jesus Christ did not give up any of His Divine attributes while here on earth. He exercised His **voluntary disuse** of His Divine attributes for His own personal convenience and purposes. He could have turned the stones into bread, but He did not. At the same time, He turned the five loaves and two fishes into food enough to feed 5,000 men plus women and children and have food left over. He healed blind eyes. He raised people from the dead. He performed many other miracles using his Divine attributes of omnipotence, omniscience, omnipresence, and all the other attributes of Deity.

"Made Himself of no Reputation"

QUESTION #1017

What does it mean when the Bible says that the Lord Jesus Christ *"made himself of no reputation"*?

ANSWER #1017

In the King James Bible, Philippians 2:6-8 reads:

> *"Who, being in the form of God, thought it not robbery to be equal with God: But __made himself of no reputation__, and took upon him the form of a servant, and was made in the likeness of men: And being found in fashion as a man, he humbled himself, and became obedient unto death, even the death of the cross."*

The words, *"made himself of no reputation,"* are a translation of one Greek verb, KENOO. The noun that comes from this verb forms a theological term. It is called the KENOSIS. This means that He gave up the voluntary use of His Divine attributes for His own personal use. The mere disuse of those Divine attributes does not deny that He still possessed them. He was Perfect Man and Perfect God. He possessed all the attributes of Deity. He did not lack a single one.

Why Christ's Incarnation?

QUESTION #1018

Since God the Father has no blood, is this why the Lord Jesus Christ needed to take on Himself human flesh in order for Him to have blood that could be shed for the remission of sins?

ANSWER #1018

That is certainly one reason for the need for the miraculous incarnation of the Lord Jesus Christ. He also had to experience in his Perfect human body the various testings and temptations that human beings live through so that He could be a faithful and merciful High Priest.

. The Crucifixion and Resurrection

QUESTION #1019

Is it right to believe that Jesus was crucified on Passover Nisan (April) 14 and raised on 16 Nisan-April?

ANSWER #1019

It would be wrong to have the crucifixion on the 14th of the month and to have the resurrection of the Lord Jesus Christ on the 16th of the month. As the

Lord Jesus Christ Himself stated about how long He was in the tomb:

Matthew 12:40

*"For **as** Jonas was **three days and three nights** in the whale's belly; **so** shall the Son of man be **three days and three nights** in the heart of the earth."*

I believe we should take "three days and three nights" in a literal fashion. This comes to 72 hours. From the 14th to the 16th could not possibly be 72 hours. Therefore these dates cannot be Biblical.

Remembering the Resurrection

QUESTION #1020

Are we to remember the bodily resurrection only on the day that some refer to as "*Easter*" Sunday?

ANSWER #1020

You can remember the bodily resurrection of the Lord Jesus Christ on any day of the year. Many of the ministers in the churches that celebrate "*Easter*" services (though they don't necessarily come out and tell the people about it) do not believe in the bodily resurrection of the Lord Jesus Christ. They believe that He rose only in spirit, not in His glorified body. They are therefore heretics on this issue.

How Can a Person Be "Saved"

QUESTION #1021

How is a person "*saved*" and become a member of God's family?

ANSWER #1021

For people to be genuinely born-again, saved, and become a member of God's family they must (1) realize that they are a sinner in God's eyes; (2) realize that the Lord Jesus Christ died for their sins and is able to save them; and (3) genuinely accept, receive, and believe on the Lord Jesus Christ as their Saviour. You should look up, read carefully, and understand each of the following verses: John 1:10-12; 3:16-17; 3:36; 5:24; Romans 3:23; 6:23; and 1 Peter 2:24.

Is Eternal Security Biblical?

QUESTION #1022

I am also in the process of writing a book refuting "*conditional security.*" What is your view on this?

ANSWER #1022

I do not believe in only "*conditional security*" for the born-again Christian. I do not believe one who is genuinely born-again can be un-born-again spiritually, any more than a person who has been physically born can be un-born physically. It is possible for a person to be disobedient as a son or daughter, but he or she remains a son or daughter.

I believe John 10:27-30 tells the story fully:

> "*My sheep hear my voice, and I know them, and they follow me: And **I give unto them eternal life; and they shall never perish, neither shall any man pluck them out of my hand**. 29 My Father, which gave them me, is greater than all; and no man is able to pluck them out of my Father's hand. 30 I and my Father are one.*"

According to these verses, the Lord Jesus Christ Himself said of His "*sheep*," that these who are genuinely saved, and born-again people can "*never perish*" nor "*shall any man pluck them out of My hand.*"

Needing Assurance of Salvation

QUESTION #1023

Am I saved? I believe that Jesus died on the cross for my sins and that He has forgiven me for my many sins as I have asked forgiveness. That does not mean we don't suffer the consequences of sin or still have open doors for attack from the enemy. I have asked Jesus to come into my heart and save me. I have been baptized in Jesus' name. I try to study the Bible. What else can I do?

ANSWER #1023

I am glad that you want to be sure that you are saved. I would just ask you a few questions: (1) Have you had a change of mind regarding sin? Do you agree that God considers you to be a sinner? Do you agree you can't save yourself? (2) Have you had a change of mind regarding the Saviour? Do you believe that the Lord Jesus Christ died for all your sins? Do you believe that He and He alone can save your soul from Hell? (3) Have you genuinely received Him, accepted Him, and believed on Him as your Saviour Who alone can save you? If all these things are true concerning you, you can claim God's promises in both John 1:10-13 and John 3:16 (which say that you are born-again, saved, and have everlasting life).

John 1:10-13

"He was in the world, and the world was made by him, and the world knew him not. He came unto his own, and his own received him not. But as many __as received him, to them gave he power to become the sons of God, even to them that believe on his name: Which were born__, not of blood, nor of the will of the flesh, nor of the will of man, but __of God__."

John 3:16

"For God so loved the world, that he gave his only begotten Son, that __whosoever believeth in him should not perish, but have everlasting life__."

"Jehovah" Versus "Yahweh"

QUESTION #1024

Where do you think Christians got the name of "*Yahweh*"?

ANSWER #1024

I believe they got it from putting the wrong vowels under the Hebrew consonants YHWH. They are not the vowel points used in our Masoretic Traditional Hebrew Text. The proper Name for the Lord in the Old Testament is "*Jehovah*," not "*Yahweh*."

Proper Biblical Interpretation

QUESTION #1025

I have been debating with a friend of mine who is a Calvinist and a partial preterist. I have been challenging him on how he finds merit in the Scriptures to allegorize away so much of prophesy in the Bible. When I talk about a literal fulfilment of Revelation, he says to me: "*You believe that the sun and moon will be darkened as it says in Revelation?*" I answer "*Yes.*" He says that this type of imagery is all through the Old Testament where none of it was ever fulfilled literally. He wonders why I believe that it will be fulfilled literally in Revelation. I would like your help on answering this objection .

ANSWER #1025

In answer to your friend's question about literal interpretation, I would refer you to a good statement about Bible interpretation. It goes something like this:

> *"When the plain sense of Scripture makes common sense, seek no other sense. Therefore, take every word at its primary, ordinary, usual, literal meaning, unless the facts*

of the immediate context, studied in the light of related passages, and axiomatic and fundamental truths, indicate clearly otherwise. God, in revealing His Word, neither intends nor permits the reader to be confused. He wants His children to understand." (Quoted from page xxiv of the *Defined King James Bible*, Author Unknown)

Since your friend looks like both a hyper-Calvinist and a Preterist, you might as well give up on him in the area of Bible interpretation. Both these beliefs involve elements that are extremely heretical. I wonder if you should waste any more of your time even discussing things with him unless and until you can see he is open to change his position in light of truth and facts.

The Beginning of the Church
QUESTION #1026

I hear that some people believe that the church started before the day of Pentecost. When did the church begin?

ANSWER #1026

Though the Lord Jesus Christ is the foundation of the church, I believe the church, the body of Christ, began on the day of Pentecost after the Lord Jesus Christ, its Head, died for the sins of the world at Calvary, ascended to Heaven, and sent the Holy Spirit to empower the church. I believe that those who teach the church began either with John the Baptist or in the days when the Lord Jesus Christ was on earth are in error.

New Revelation and Mormonism
QUESTION #1027

I was doing some reading about the Mormon Church and thought about how there are some similarities to the charismatic church. For instance, the charismatic doctrine is the New Apostolic Reformation (NAR), where they think modern-day apostles and prophets are being raised up to re-establish the fivefold ministry of Ephesians 4:11-12. These "new" apostles and prophets receive "*new revelation.*" It this Biblical?

ANSWER #1027

An interesting comparison between these two false cults. The teaching that there are modern "*apostles and prophets*" is not Biblical. These offices passed off the scene with the passing of the apostolic age. Regarding "*new revelation,*" Peter Ruckman, Gail Riplinger, and their followers believe this false concept. They believe and teach that the King James Bible is a "*new*

> *revelation*" which was "*God-breathed*" or "*inspired of God*." They teach that
> this "*new revelation*" replaces God's only true revelation in the Hebrew,
> Aramaic, and Greek Words of the Bible.

The Church, the Body of Christ
QUESTION #1028

In reflecting over Dr. Strouse's view on the Doctrine of the Church, I wonder if he would prefer to have a Bible which was translated only by his church? How does he reconcile the fact that the King James Bible was produced by a wide variety of Bible believers from different walks of faith? I read on his website that he only supports missionaries that are of his church, and/or graduates of his seminary. His position being, I think, one of an extreme Baptist, who does not fellowship with anyone but his own immediate church family. I do believe that we Baptists ought not to think of ourselves as the sole Body of Christ, as this would certainly fall under Baptist-bridism, or Baptist-bodyism. I do, however, believe that other Bible-believers compose the Body of Christ. Is this pretty much what you were referring to in regards to Dr. Strouse's views?

ANSWER #1028

You are right about those who produced the King James Bible. They were Church of England Anglicans, not Baptists. You are correct in emphasizing the local churches, as the Bible does, but we must affirm that all saved people make up the body of Christ, not just Baptists. This is what I have against Dr. Strouse's position though there are many things we agree upon.

Cults–7th Day Adventism
QUESTION #1029

I have recently had a conversation with a Seventh Day Adventist that comes into my place of business. I always thought I could shoot them down because I understood that they would have to keep the whole Law, in other words, they couldn't kindle any fire throughout their habitation on the Sabbath. So to keep the law, they would have to observe "*all things*" and if they did keep the whole Law and yet offend in any, then they were "*guilty of all*" at least that's how I read my King James Bible . This individual is trying to say that we should observe the Sabbath and he's taking me to the book of John chapter 14 verse 15 "*If ye love me, keep my commandments*."

I know he's not right concerning the Sabbath but what is the Scripture saying here? Most all of my dealings with false doctrine/cults is that they mix a little truth with serious error. I need help with this one, if you have the time. Could you tell me what "*commandments*" mean in the context of John chapter

14 verse 15? Also, how would you handle this person? How is he wrong in using this passage to promote his teachings? I understand that you are busy but this would help me greatly.

ANSWER #1029

I have attached in PDF "*1,050 commands in the New Testament for Christians to obey.*" None of the Old Testament commandments are for us, only those in the New Testament. I think this will help you with this discussion. However, don't be surprised if your Seventh Day Adventist man will not listen. They are very much indoctrinated in their errors.

Use of Divorced People in Church

QUESTION #1030

I wondered if you could give me some counsel on how people who have been divorced can be used in the Church. For instance, I realize they are not to be ministers or deacons, but I wondered about other roles. For instance, can someone with divorce in their background lead a small Bible study--for instance, a female with females during the week? Can they be a Sunday school teacher for children? Let's say that the persons tried their best to save their marriage, but one person left anyway. Also, at one time, I talked with you about the issue of remarriage and I got some of your materials from the Bible For Today. Those articles mentioned that if a person had been divorced and remarried, he or she should try to go back to the original spouse. Do you still hold to that teaching?

ANSWER #1030

There is no definite answer on this question except for pastors and deacons mentioned clearly in 1 Timothy and Titus. These officers must be "*the husband of one wife*" and therefore not divorced and remarried or remarried while his wife is still living. Here are a few things to consider as far as service in the local church by someone who has been divorced and remarried:
1. the person should not be in leadership positions.
2. females teaching females (if they understand the situation and accept it) might be all right.
3. teaching children might be a bad example.
4. church clerk might be all right.
5. attendance at all services of the church should be urged.
6. helping to clean the church would be fine.
7. in places where there would be no temptation either to the person, or to others to act or think unbiblically toward each other.

1 Corinthians 7:11 says this about a wife who has departed from her husband:

> "*But and if she depart, let her remain unmarried, or be reconciled to her husband: and let not the husband put away his wife.*"

If it is possible for a person to get back with their original spouse, it's worth a try, though it is not always possible. I still believe this because it is taught clearly in 1 Corinthians 7:11.

Returning to Mate After Divorce

QUESTION #1031

When you say a divorced person should go back to his or her mate, would this include someone going back to the original spouse, if possible, even though they had married again? I want to make sure I'm understanding this correctly. When you mention teaching children, are you talking about a formal position of teaching children in Sunday school in a church? There would be grandchildren of which divorced Christian people would probably be teaching things about the Bible, I would think.

ANSWER #1031

It would be a little difficult to go back if the spouse had married again. I would think teaching grandchildren the Bible things would certainly be proper. The Lord must lead you in any of these activities. The Bible is not specific in these matters, so I cannot be either. We should not stumble fellow believers in any way, though this is not always easy. We must serve the Lord with gladness in whatever He leads us to do.

The Sadness of Divorce

QUESTION #1032

My wife cheated on me and left last year. It wasn't my fault. I was faithful. Should I remain single for the rest of my life? I am an only child and I am all alone. My parents are in their 60's, so I will really be alone in the years or decades to come. I have no family, and I want a family. I am a veteran, and I put myself through college, I went to church my whole life. I try to do everything right.

ANSWER #1032

I am very sorry for your situation. <u>Your wife has sinned greatly both in adultery and in forsaking her husband.</u> If there is a way to reconcile with her and bring her back, that would be the Biblical answer. You would have to forgive her, she would have to repent of her sin and clean up her life, and then you two could go on together. She might be willing to come back. She might also have some conditions that you would have to meet for her to return. You should be willing to meet those conditions in order to have her back. You will do what you want to do about this, <u>but as a faithful pastor, I must preach what the Bible says about marriage so that young people and others who are getting married will know what God's standard is.</u> Perhaps some, if not all, might hearken to His way and will. Here are some of the verses on divorce and remarriage:

> Mark 10:11 *"And he saith unto them, Whosoever shall put away his wife, and marry another, committeth adultery against her."*
> Luke 16:18 *"Whosoever putteth away his wife, and marrieth another, committeth adultery: and whosoever marrieth her that is put away from her husband committeth adultery."*
> 1 Corinthians 7:10-11 *"And unto the married I command, yet not I, but the Lord, Let not the wife depart from her husband: But and if she depart, let her remain unmarried, or be reconciled to her husband: and let not the husband put away his wife."*
> Romans 7:2-3 *"For the woman which hath an husband is bound by the law to her husband so long as he liveth; but if the husband be dead, she is loosed from the law of her husband. So then if, while her husband liveth, she be married to another man, she shall be called an adulteress: but if her husband be dead, she is free from that law; so that she is no adulteress, though she be married to another man."*

Regarding the spouse committing adultery, that is a sad situation indeed. The spouse would be wrong, and committing sin, but Christian Biblical marriage is still for life until the death of the spouse. Your service to our country is commendable. It is sad that veterans must leave their families so often. This breaks them apart. I was a Navy Chaplain with 5 years active duty. One of them was in Okinawa without the family, so I know it is difficult.

Divorce & Remarriage Questions
QUESTION #1033

Thank you also for the sermonaudio.com message on *"Divorce and Remarriage"* which I have listened to. This has been the answer I have been anticipating. Your answer confirms what others have also said. I needed to be sure from someone, as yourself, who has an impeccable degree of knowledge about the Greek language. This has cleared up everything of what I was uncertain of. Please, if I may, I would like to ask you another question. If a man, who has never been married before, marries a woman who has been divorced, they would be living in adultery. This marriage would obviously not be recognized in the sight of God. If that man realized the mistake he had made by marrying the divorced woman, and dissolved the adulterous union, could he be free to marry again, that is, to a woman who has not been married before?

ANSWER #1033

It is true that this man would have committed adultery according to the clear teaching of Mark, Luke, Romans 7, and 1 Corinthians 7. I have never been asked this question before. I suppose if he dissolved the adulterous marriage once he was convicted of it, he might be able to marry a virgin or a widow, but since he was *"married"* before, the virgin or widow who marries him might be committing adultery. It's something to ponder. It is not completely clear.

The Jewish "Betrothal" Custom
QUESTION #1034

This subject, I believe, is a matter of great importance to the spiritual well being of the church. Because it is such a sensitive issue due to its emotionally direct involvement in the lives of a man and a woman who want to marry despite whether divorce in a previous marriage has resulted or not in their lives. Some pastors are not addressing the issue from a Biblical standpoint or what God has said about divorce and remarriage in His Word. Therefore, controversy is avoided in order to keep the peace. It is important for me to know exactly how to understand what Jesus taught, in comparison to what Paul said in respect of divorce and remarriage. Imparting this knowledge will be my gain as well as those I can bless with it.

ANSWER #1034

The Lord Jesus Christ's teaching in Matthew 5 and 19 refers to the Jewish custom of betrothal. This is because Matthew was the Gospel especially given to the Jews. Therefore, Jewish customs and practices were in view. During this betrothal period used by the Jews, the man and woman, though not married, and though without any sexual union, were called "husband" and "wife" as were Joseph and Mary. If either party was unfaithful during this time due to fornication ("*saving for the cause of fornication*"), the one party could divorce the other. Only in the betrothal period could a divorce be honored.

On the other hand, the Gospels of Mark, Luke, Paul's letters of Romans 7, and 1 Corinthians 7 are crystal clear that only death breaks a marriage–and nothing else. I have e-mailed you my sermon on *"Divorce and Remarriage"* where I go into the details on this question. I think this will clear this up for you.

The Bible and Suicide
QUESTION #1035

I have a very important question that I have not heard one person preach on. That is suicide. I have a two-part question.
1. What happens when a lost or unsaved person commits suicide and dies?
2. What happens when or "if" a "born-again" Bible believing Christian commits suicide and dies? If this Christian believed on Christ's sacrifice by faith and was born-again with the Holy Spirit of promise, and repented towards God in genuine faith, and yet commits suicide later on, because of whatever reason, will that Christian still go to Heaven and be present with the Lord then?

ANSWER #1035
1.   This unsaved person is sent to Hell in the lake of fire, for eternity. He will be judged at the Great White Throne judgment.
2.   This born-again, saved person, will be sent to Heaven. He will be judged at the Judgment Seat of Christ in a righteous way. He cannot lose his salvation if he were genuinely saved, no matter how much he walked after his flesh.

Tongues and Pentecostalism
QUESTION #1036

I was thrown out of the United Pentecostal Church because of a hair and skirt issue. I think the real reason was my opposition to some of their holidays. The leaders encouraged me to ask for the gift of speaking in tongues because, for them, that was evidence of being filled with the Holy Spirit. So I tried to practice it. It sounded like gibberish to me and was not coming naturally. After they told me to leave, I stopped trying. I will try to listen to your message again. Are you saying it is wrong to speak in tongues?

ANSWER #1036

Yes, I am saying it is unscriptural to speak in tongues. The nine sign gifts ceased after the completion of the New Testament in 90 or 100 A.D. I do not believe the present speaking tongues are of God, but are either of the flesh or of the Devil, or both.

Belief in a Literal Hell

QUESTION #1037

How many people really believe there is a Hell.

ANSWER #1037

Though there are no complete figures on this question, I am sorry to say that there are very few people who believe there is a real everlasting Hell with literal fire which was "***prepared for the Devil and his angels***." However, this denial of the Bible's Hell does not take away its reality. The Bible is clear that those who have not genuinely received the Lord Jesus Christ as their Saviour from their sins will go to that place where the "*Devil and his angels*" will be sent. The words, "***should not perish***" in John 3:16 refer to the fires of Hell. The escape from Hell is taught clearly in this verse. It is for "***whosoever believeth in Him***."

Matthew 25:41

"*Then shall he say also unto them on the left hand, Depart from me, ye cursed, into **everlasting fire, prepared for the devil and his angels**:*"

John 3:16

"*For God so loved the world, that he gave his only begotten Son, that whosoever believeth in him **should not perish**, but have everlasting life.*"

Eternal Security Is Biblical

QUESTION #1038

What line do you take on the eternal security of the Believer?

ANSWER #1038

I side with the Lord Jesus Christ on eternal security as found in John 10:27-30:

"*My sheep hear my voice, and I know them, and they follow me: And **I give unto them eternal life; and they shall never perish, neither shall any man pluck them out of my hand**. My Father, which gave them me, is greater than all; and no man is able to pluck them out of my Father's hand. I and my Father are one.*"

British Israelism's Errors

QUESTION #1039

What does British Israelism teach? Is it Biblical?

ANSWER #1039

I am opposed to British Israelism. It goes along with the idea that some or all of the 10 tribes that returned from the Assyrian captivity were really the white Anglo Saxon people who are now the real "Jews." This view teaches that Britain, America, Germany, and other white nations are the real Jews and the other "Jews" are impostors. I believe this view is held by the Mormons. It leads to white supremacy and in some cases to Nazi views with hatred for the Jews. This is behind what is called British Israelism. I have written 20 pages on this British Israelism cult as referenced below. It is called *"British Israelism Exposed"* **(BFT #990, 20 pages @ $4.00 + $2.00 S&H)**.

CHAPTER II
QUESTIONS ABOUT
THE OLD TESTAMENT

Manasseh or Moses?
QUESTION #1040
I came across a Commentary that says the following:
Judges 18:30 "It is generally admitted that, in Judges, for 'Manasseh' (King James Bible, NASB) we should read 'Moses' . . ."
I wondered what your thoughts were on this.
ANSWER #1040
This commentary comment is a heresy. The Hebrew text reads clearly, "MANASSEH" and not "MOSES."

Hebrew or Dead Sea Scrolls?
QUESTION #1041
My question is, what can I refer to if I can't refer to the Dead Sea Scrolls which are the earliest scriptures I am aware of? Is there another source I can refer to when refuting the common "the Bible was edited" argument?
ANSWER #1041
You should not rely for anything on the Dead Sea Scrolls. They are perverted copies of the Old Testament by the Essenes cult. They should never be used to refute the Masoretic Hebrew text that underlies the King James Bible.

The Tabernacle of David
QUESTION #1042
I have an Old Testament Question that is brought up in the New Testament in the Book of Acts. What is the Tabernacle of David? Does it have anything to do with us today?

ANSWER #1042
Acts 15:16
"*After this I will return, and will build again __the tabernacle of David__, which is fallen down; and I will build again the ruins thereof, and I will set it up:*"

From Isaiah 16:5, Amos 9:11, and Acts 15:16, this refers to the reinstitution of the establishment of Israel's prominence which will take place in the millennial reign of the Lord Jesus Christ when He returns after the seven year Tribulation period to set up His kingdom reign.

The Ark Of The Covenant
QUESTION #1043
I do not understand why King David brought the Ark of the Covenant up to Jerusalem to Mount Moriah and did not return it to its rightful place in the Tabernacle of Moses at Gibeon.

ANSWER #1043
2 Samuel 6:1 and following, shows that David sought to bring up the ark in the wrong way. It was on a "*new cart*" rather than on the shoulders of the priests. 2 Samuel 6:9 says that David was afraid to bring the ark to Jerusalem, so he left it in the house of Obededom. After 3 months, David brought it the proper way to Jerusalem.

Jeremiah 10:5 Version Differences
QUESTION #1044
Jeremiah 10:5
King James Bible
"*They are upright as the __palm tree__, but speak not:*"
New American Standard And New International
"*Like a scarecrow in a __cucumber field__ are they, And they cannot speak*";

Can you explain what happened with this verse that appears so different in the King James Bible from the NASV and NIV? I wondered if the NASV and NIV used a different Hebrew text or whether they just translated it differently.

ANSWER #1044
TOMER is the Hebrew Word behind the King James Bible in the Logos Bible Program. It is translated "*palm tree*" in the King James Bible. It is translated either "cucumber tree" as in the NASV, or "melon patch" as in the NIV.

Since it looks like this is the only time TOMER occurs in the Old Testament, I would rely upon the expertise of the King James Bible translators in comparing the various cognate and sister languages and coming up with this meaning of "palm tree" rather than relying on the far less qualified assessment of the modern translators either of the NASV or the NIV who arrive at two different meanings of TOMER.

Water Out of the Rock

QUESTION #1045
Exodus 17:5-6

*"And the LORD said unto Moses, Go on before the people, and take with thee of the elders of Israel; and thy rod, wherewith thou smotest the river, take in thine hand, and go. Behold, I will stand before thee there upon the rock in Horeb; and **thou shalt smite the rock**, and there shall come water out of it, that the people may drink. And Moses did so in the sight of the elders of Israel."*

If in Exodus 17:5-6 God told Moses to **strike the rock** for water, why was he punished for disobedience when he **struck the rock** for water in Numbers 20:8?

Numbers 20:8-11

*"**Take the rod**, and gather thou the assembly together, thou, and Aaron thy brother, and **speak ye unto the rock** before their eyes; and it shall give forth his water, and thou shalt bring forth to them water out of the rock: so thou shalt give the congregation and their beasts drink. And Moses took the rod from before the LORD, as he commanded him. And Moses and Aaron gathered the congregation together before the rock, and he said unto them, Hear now, ye rebels; must we fetch you water out of this rock? And Moses lifted up his hand, and **with his rod he smote the rock twice**: and the water came out abundantly, and the congregation drank, and their beasts also."*

ANSWER #1045

These are two completely separate incidents. There is no contradiction in any way here. In the first incident, Moses obeyed the Lord and smote the rock. In the second, Moses disobeyed the Lord because he was told **to speak** to the rock, and instead **he smote it**, not once, but **twice**. He was also quite nasty to the Israelites in his words when he said, *"Hear now, ye rebels; must we fetch you water out of this rock?"* Psalm 106:33 explains how God viewed Moses' words on that occasion:

Psalm 106:33

*"Because they provoked his spirit, so that **he spake unadvisedly with his lips**."*

Why Include Aramaic In O.T.?

QUESTION #1046

I couldn't help but notice the emphasis on the languages of the underlying text changing from time to time in your video. You at some times, I believe, said they were Hebrew and Greek but most of the time you said they were Hebrew, Aramaic, and Greek. Why did you include the Aramaic?

ANSWER #1046

Hebrew, Aramaic, and Greek Words refer to the Words underlying the King James Bible. Though there are very few verses in the Old Testament in Aramaic, I must include that language as the basis for our King James Bible. The following quotation shows the verses in the Old Testament that are written in Aramaic:

*"Apart from two short passages, (**Genesis 31:47 and Jeremiah 10:11**) **Ezra 4:8-6:18; 7:12-26; and Daniel 2:4-7:28** are the portions of the Old Testament that are written in Aramaic. The rationale for the two sections of Ezra that are in Aramaic is easy to determine. These are the passages that deal with official correspondence regarding the rebuilding of the temple in Jerusalem under the auspices of Darius and Artaxerxes (**Ezra 4:8; 5:6**) and the mission of Ezra under the auspices of King Artaxerxes (**Ezra 7:11**)."*

http://www.studylight.org/ls/at/index.cgi?a=189

More About Aramaic O.T. & N.T.

QUESTION #1047

What language were those few words in Daniel written in? Was it Aramaic, Chaldean, or Syraic? Did the people of the New Testament speak Aramaic?

ANSWER #1047

Old Testament Aramaic is sometimes called "Chaldee." It is also sometimes called "Syrian." The article on "Biblical Aramaic" from *Wikipedia* has some of the following information. There are a few Aramaic words in the New Testament as well.

> "Biblical Aramaic *is the form of the Aramaic language that is used in the books of Daniel, Ezra, and a few other places in the Hebrew Bible and should not be confused with the Aramaic translations of the Hebrew Bible known as targumim*."

Chaldee language

> "*The language used by the sacred writers in certain portions of the Old Testament, viz., Dan. 2:4-7, 28; Ezra 4:8-6:18; 7:12-26; Gen. 31:46; Jer. 10:11. It is the Aramaic dialect, as it is sometimes called, as distinguished from the Hebrew dialect. It was the language of commerce and of social intercourse in Western Asia, and after the Exile gradually came to be the popular language of Palestine. It is called "Syrian" in 2 Kings 18:26. Some isolated words in this language are preserved in the New Testament (Matt. 5:22; 6:24; 16:17; 27:46; Mark 3:17; 5:41; 7:34; 14:36; Acts 1:19; 1 Cor. 16:22). These are specimens of the vernacular language of Palestine at that period. The term "Hebrew" was also sometimes applied to the Chaldee because it had become the language of the Hebrews (John 5:2; 19:20)*."

Old Testament "Sheol"

QUESTION #1048

I have a question about a comment in a book I have been using in class. The author claims the Hebrew word, SHEOL, is translated "*grave*" 31 times in the Authorized Version and 31 times "*hell*." He claims this is an error. He claims that "Sheol" is never the grave.

ANSWER #1048

I would simply say that SHEOL is the place of departed spirits in the Old Testament. The context would determine whether it refers to the place where the body was laid which would be the "*grave*," or where the spirit and soul went which would either be "*paradise*" (the blessed section of SHEOL) or "*hell*" (the damned section of SHEOL). The King James Bible interpreted these verses properly so far as I know. I wouldn't argue with this man. If that's all he has against the King James Bible, it's a small thing. I'm sure he has many other things against it as well.

"Wine" in the Old Testament

QUESTION #1049

I'm in an in-depth Bible study on the Book of Jeremiah. In Jeremiah 35:2, I looked up the word "*wine*" and the reference material said it was fermented wine, "YAYIN." Is the reference material correct that it is fermented wine? Would God tell them to drink something that He warns people not to drink in other passages?

ANSWER #1049

Whether the word, "*wine*," in the King James Bible (whether it is translating the Hebrew word, YAYIN, or the Greek word, OINOS) is fermented or not fermented depends entirely on the context. Sometimes it is fermented and sometimes it is not. The book, *Wines in the Bible–The Laws Of Fermentation* (**BFT #514 @ $7.00 + $3.00 S&H**) makes this clear and shows it to be true.

Various Old Testament Questions

QUESTION #1050

1.   Who was Nehemiah? Was he a prophet or a priest?
2.   Who came first, King Cyrus or King Darius as mentioned in Ezra and Nehemiah?
3.   If a person is unsaved and belongs to Satan, does God still love that unbeliever even though he is lost?
4.   What Scripture is there to back up either claim?

ANSWER #1050

1.   Some say Nehemiah was a priest. I am not certain. Ezra was definitely a priest as well as a scribe (Ezra 7:11.)

2.   Cyrus was the king of Persia. It says in Ezra 4:5:

"*And hired counsellers against them, to frustrate their purpose, all the days of **Cyrus king of Persia**, even until the reign of **Darius king of Persia**.*"

From this verse, it looks like Cyrus was first and Darius was second as King of Persia.

3.   God still loves the unbelievers, even though he hates iniquity of all kinds.

4.   One Scripture that backs this up is John 3:16. It shows that God loved the entire world of people enough to send His only begotten Son to die for their sins.

"*For **God so loved the world**, that he gave his only begotten Son, that whosoever believeth in him should not perish, but have everlasting life.*"

Hebrew Versus the Dead Sea Scrolls
QUESTION #1051

I was speaking to a fellow Christian who said the Dead Sea Scrolls are okay to use to show that the Old Testament Bible has not been changed. I told him that the Essenes cult is supposed to have changed the Old Testament Words. He asked me in what book this is found. He said that, from what he currently knows about it, he does not believe this is true. I was unable to tell him exactly what is corrupted since I don't know myself. Can you give me a few examples of the changes or even direct me to an online article that expounds on it?

ANSWER #1051

I think one way for you to find deviations from the Old Testament Hebrew Words as suggested by the Dead Sea Scrolls would be for you to do the following things: (1) buy or borrow a New International Version (NIV); (2) look at all the Old Testament footnotes; (3) observe when the NIV suggests changing the Hebrew Words in the text for some other words advocated by the Dead Sea Scrolls. In that way, you can collect for yourself many such examples with which to answer your friend. You are correct about the heretical Essenes. You are also correct about the inferiority of the Dead Sea Scrolls. Though the NIV and other versions have done so, I do not believe anyone should ever take a Dead Sea Scroll reading in place of the Traditional Hebrew Words that underlie the King James Bible.

Daniel 9:25-29 And "Messiah"
QUESTION #1052

Recently I was told that the King James Bible translation of Daniel 9:25-26 was incorrect where it reads the "*Messiah.*" The opinion of many is that it should have been translated "*anointed*" as in most versions. Can you shed some light on the passage?

ANSWER #1052
In Daniel 9:25-26, the King James Bible accurately **transliterates**, letter for letter, MESSIAH. The **translation** of that word is "*anointed*" but the King James Bible chose not to **translate** but to **transliterate**, that is put it letter for letter. That is exactly the Hebrew Word. Tell the one who told you this is an error, that they are wrong.

Old Testament Capital Punishment
QUESTION #1053
Can you think of a Biblical example of a civil government practicing the death penalty for adultery, or homosexuality, or any sin?
ANSWER #1053
Here are many examples from the Old Testament under the law of Moses where the **death penalty** was demanded. However, it must be made clear that we today are no longer under Moses' law, but are now in the dispensation of the grace of God. All these **death penalties** do not apply in our New Testament era.

Numbers 15:32-36
"*And while the children of Israel were in the wilderness, they found a man that gathered sticks upon the sabbath day. And they that found him gathering sticks brought him unto Moses and Aaron, and unto all the congregation. And they put him in ward, because it was not declared what should be done to him. And the LORD said unto Moses, The man shall be surely put to death: all the congregation shall stone him with stones without the camp. And all the congregation brought him without the camp, and stoned him with stones, and he died; as the LORD commanded Moses.*"

Exodus 21:12
"*He that smiteth a man, so that he die, shall be surely put to death.*"

Exodus 21:15
"*And he that smiteth his father, or his mother, shall be surely put to death.*"

Exodus 21:16
"*And he that stealeth a man, and selleth him, or if he be found in his hand, he shall surely be put to death.*"

Exodus 21:17

"And he that curseth his father, or his mother, shall surely be __put to death__."

Exodus 21:29

"But if the ox were wont to push with his horn in time past, and it hath been testified to his owner, and he hath not kept him in, but that he hath killed a man or a woman; the ox shall be stoned, and his owner also shall be __put to death__."

Exodus 22:19

"Whosoever lieth with a beast shall surely be __put to death__."

Exodus 31:14

"Ye shall keep the sabbath therefore; for it is holy unto you: every one that defileth it shall surely be __put to death__: for whosoever doeth any work therein, that soul shall be cut off from among his people."

Exodus 31:15

"Six days may work be done; but in the seventh is the sabbath of rest, holy to the LORD: whosoever doeth any work in the sabbath day, he shall surely be __put to death__."

Exodus 35:2

"Six days shall work be done, but on the seventh day there shall be to you an holy day, a sabbath of rest to the LORD: whosoever doeth work therein shall be __put to death__."

Leviticus 20:2

"Again, thou shalt say to the children of Israel, Whosoever he be of the children of Israel, or of the strangers that sojourn in Israel, that giveth any of his seed unto Molech; he shall surely be __put to death__: the people of the land shall stone him with stones."

Leviticus 20:9

"For every one that curseth his father or his mother shall be surely __put to death__: he hath cursed his father or his mother; his blood shall be upon him."

Leviticus 20:10

"*And the man that committeth adultery with another man's wife, even he that committeth adultery with his neighbour's wife, the adulterer and the adulteress shall surely be __put to death__.*"

Leviticus 20:11

"*And the man that lieth with his father's wife hath uncovered his father's nakedness: both of them shall surely be __put to death__; their blood shall be upon them.*"

Leviticus 20:12

"*And if a man lie with his daughter in law, both of them shall surely be __put to death__: they have wrought confusion; their blood shall be upon them.*"

Leviticus 20:13

"*If a man also lie with mankind, as he lieth with a woman, both of them have committed an abomination: they shall surely be __put to death__; their blood shall be upon them.*"

Leviticus 20:15

"*And if a man lie with a beast, he shall surely be __put to death__: and ye shall slay the beast.*"

Leviticus 20:16

"*And if a woman approach unto any beast, and lie down thereto, thou shalt kill the woman, and the beast: they shall surely be __put to death__; their blood shall be upon them.*"

Leviticus 20:27

"*A man also or woman that hath a familiar spirit, or that is a wizard, shall surely be __put to death__: they shall stone them with stones: their blood shall be upon them.*"

Leviticus 24:16

"*And he that blasphemeth the name of the LORD, he shall surely be __put to death__, and all the congregation shall certainly stone him: as well the stranger, as he that is born in the land, when he blasphemeth the name of the LORD, shall be __put to death__.*"

Leviticus 24:17

"*And he that killeth any man shall surely be __put to death__.*"

Leviticus 24:21
*"And he that killeth a beast, he shall restore it: and he that killeth a man, he shall be **put to death**."*

Numbers 1:51
"And when the tabernacle setteth forward, the Levites shall take it down: and when the tabernacle is to be

*pitched, the Levites shall set it up: and the stranger that cometh nigh shall be **put to death**."*

Numbers 3:10
*"And thou shalt appoint Aaron and his sons, and they shall wait on their priest's office: and the stranger that cometh nigh shall be **put to death**."*

Numbers 3:38
*"But those that encamp before the tabernacle toward the east, even before the tabernacle of the congregation eastward, shall be Moses, and Aaron and his sons, keeping the charge of the sanctuary for the charge of the children of Israel; and the stranger that cometh nigh shall be **put to death**."*

Numbers 15:32-36
*"And while the children of Israel were in the wilderness, they found a man that gathered sticks upon the sabbath day. And they that found him gathering sticks brought him unto Moses and Aaron, and unto all the congregation. And they put him in ward, because it was not declared what should be done to him. And the LORD said unto Moses, The man shall be surely **put to death**: all the congregation shall stone him with stones without the camp. And all the congregation brought him without the camp, and stoned him with stones, and **he died**; as the LORD commanded Moses."*

Numbers 18:7
*"Therefore thou and thy sons with thee shall keep your priest's office for every thing of the altar, and within the vail; and ye shall serve: I have given your priest's office unto you as a service of gift: and the stranger that cometh nigh shall be **put to death**."*

Numbers 35:16
*"And if he smite him with an instrument of iron, so that he die, he is a murderer: the murderer shall surely be **put to death**."*

Numbers 35:17
*"And if he smite him with throwing a stone, wherewith he may die, and he die, he is a murderer: the murderer shall surely be **put to death**."*

Numbers 35:18
*"Or if he smite him with an hand weapon of wood, wherewith he may die, and he die, he is a murderer: the murderer shall surely be **put to death**."*

Numbers 35:21
*"Or in enmity smite him with his hand, that he die: he that smote him shall surely be **put to death**; for he is a murderer: the revenger of blood shall slay the murderer, when he meeteth him."*

Numbers 35:30
*"Whoso killeth any person, the murderer shall be **put to death** by the mouth of witnesses: but one witness shall not testify against any person to cause him to die."*

Numbers 35:31
*"Moreover ye shall take no satisfaction for the life of a murderer, which is guilty of death: but he shall be surely **put to death**."*

Deuteronomy 13:5
*"And that prophet, or that dreamer of dreams, shall be **put to death**; because he hath spoken to turn you away from the LORD your God, which brought you out of the land of Egypt, and redeemed you out of the house of bondage, to thrust thee out of the way which the LORD thy God commanded thee to walk in. So shalt thou put the evil away from the midst of thee."*

Deuteronomy 13:9
*"But thou shalt surely kill him; thine hand shall be first upon him to **put him to death**, and afterwards the hand of all the people."*

Deuteronomy 17:6
*"At the mouth of two witnesses, or three witnesses, shall he that is worthy of death be **put to death**; but at the mouth of one witness he shall not be put to death."*

Deuteronomy 17:7

"The hands of the witnesses shall be first upon him to __put__
__him to death__, and afterward the hands of all the people.
So thou shalt put the evil away from among you."

Deuteronomy 24:16

"The fathers shall not be put to death for the children,
neither shall the children be put to death for the fathers:
every man shall be __put to death__ for his own sin."

In Genesis 9:6, there seems to be the death penalty which is trans-dispensational going throughout all the Old and New Testaments as a principle.

Genesis 9:6

"Whoso sheddeth man's blood, by man shall his blood be
shed: for in the image of God made he man."

In Romans 13, in the New Testament, capital punishment is implied for those who go against Biblical government.

Romans 13:3-4

"For rulers are not a terror to good works, but to the
evil. Wilt thou then not be afraid of the power? do that
which is good, and thou shalt have praise of the same:
For he is the minister of God to thee for good. But if thou
do that which is evil, be afraid; for __he beareth not the__
__sword in vain__: for he is the minister of God, a revenger
to execute wrath upon him that doeth evil."

The Date of the Septuagint

QUESTION #1054

Can the date of the Septuagint be proved from the canon of the Old Testament? I read that the canon of the Old Testament was determined around 4 BC. If so, then it proves that the Septuagint was written before Christ. Others say the canon of the Old Testament was determined in 90 AD. If so, how come the apostles and the believers in Acts could use and read from the Old Testament books, if the canon was not until 90AD?

ANSWER #1054

There is no proof that the Septuagint (LXX) was translated from the Hebrew Old Testament B.C. That is only speculation. While it is true that a few books of the Old Testament were translated from Hebrew to Greek B.C., no one has ever produced a B.C. copy of the entire Old Testament in Greek from Genesis through Malachi. Until they produce such a copy, I will not believe in a B.C. Septuagint (LXX). The entire Septuagint (LXX) was produced in the 200's A.D. by the Gnostic heretic, Origen. He put his LXX in the 5th column of his six-column Hexapla Bible.

This being true, the apostles could not have quoted from the LXX since it wasn't in existence until after they lived. It is quite possible that the LXX quoted from the Greek New Testament. I wouldn't let either the apostate liberals, the new evangelicals, or most of the fundamentalists deceive you into the exaltation of the Septuagint (LXX) over and above the Hebrew Words that God gave to us and that were the preserved Hebrew Words from which our King James Bible was translated.

Did Jesus Quote the Septuagint?
QUESTION #1055

I have been seeing some arguments against the King James Bible. Here is a quote that I am asking about:

*"Some scholars would contend that the Masoretic Text is a more faithful rendering of the Old Testament texts, and often cite that when compared to the Dead Sea Scrolls, they are highly accurate. However, Jesus did not quote from a text that was not yet extant, but **the Septuagint (LXX) version that was known commonly by the people of His day**."*

This quotation appears to say that Jesus quoted the Septuagint and not the Masoretic Text. Just wondering why they say this, and how to stop their mouths with truth if it be not so.

ANSWER #1055

I do not believe the Septuagint (LXX) was in existence from Genesis through Malachi in the B.C. time period, though a few books might have been in Greek. The Septuagint (LXX) came out in the 200's A.D. It was found in the 5th column of Origen's 6-column Hexapla. The Lord Jesus Christ could not have quoted from something not then in existence. The Septuagint (LXX) could have quoted from the New Testament, but the New Testament could not have quoted from the Septuagint (LXX.)

Matthew 2:6 from Septuagint?
QUESTION #1056

I have read commentators who say that Matthew 2:6 in the King James Bible is a quotation from the Septuagint (LXX) Old Testament rather than the Hebrew. I thought the Septuagint was not a reliable translation. What are your thoughts on this?

ANSWER #1056

You are correct, the Septuagint is not a *"reliable translation."* I looked up the "Septuagint (LXX)" in my copy of the *International Standard Bible Encyclopedia* (ISBE). In the article, there were many instances where they referred to the looseness of translation made by the Septuagint. In a few books there was accuracy, but in most of the books there was inaccuracy in the translation. As I have said before, the King James Bible in Matthew 2:6 could not be a quote from the Septuagint (LXX) because it was not in existence until the 200's A.D. at the time of Origen.

Living Souls vs. Living Beings
QUESTION #1057

I am a King James Bible believer. I was hoping you could help me with a question. In Genesis, Adam is called a *"living soul"* after God created him. The New King James Version (NKJV) calls Adam a *"living being."* I always point this out to NKJV users and use this text to show that Adam has a soul. However, it was pointed out to me that the King James Bible calls sea creatures *"living souls"* in Revelation 16:3. Why are fish referred to as *"living souls"* in this instance?

ANSWER #1057

The English word, *"soul"* in the King James Bible can refer either to the immaterial part of our bodies, or to a *"person"* or *"human being."* It is not exclusively used in reference to the immaterial *"soul."*

Revelation 16:3

*"And the second angel poured out his vial upon the sea;
and it became as the blood of a dead man: and every
living soul died in the sea."*

This is an example of *"soul"* referring to the living creatures of the sea.

Did Jonah Die In The Whale's Belly?
QUESTION #1058

Question for you. When we studied Jonah, did he die in the belly of the fish or what exactly happened to him? A friend said she didn't remember what happened to him, and I wrote it down that he died. It's confusing and I want to make sure what I wrote is right.

ANSWER #1058

Though there are many views on this, I believe Jonah died.

Matthew 12:40

*"For as Jonas was three days and three nights in the
whale's belly; so shall the Son of man be three days and
three nights in the heart of the earth."*

This verse likens the Lord Jesus Christ's death and burial to Jonah's being three
days and three nights in the whale's belly. I believe he died there. In the book
of Jonah, notice that he was in the *"belly of hell"* or SHEOL, the place of
departed spirits in the Old Testament. Jonah was delivered *"from corruption."*
He died, and the Lord brought him back to life by resurrection, just like He
brought to life the Lord Jesus Christ.

What About The Dead Sea Scrolls?

QUESTION #1059

Would you be so kind as to give me a short explanation, and your opinion
of the "Dead Sea Scrolls" ?

ANSWER #1059

In brief, the Dead Sea Scrolls (DSS) are not to be trusted in any way when
they contradict the Masoretic Hebrew Text underlying the KJB. The New
International Version and others in their footnotes make use of the DSS to
condemn the Hebrew reading. It so happens that the DSS (in Isaiah, for
example) are in 99% in agreement with the Hebrew, but where they differ you
should always stick with the Hebrew text underlying the KJB.

The reason for distrust of the DSS is (1) we don't know for sure WHICH
HEBREW text these Essenes took from Jerusalem. Was it exact and accurate?
(2) we don't know the METHODS they used in copying from the Hebrew texts
that they had. They might have been very sloppy.

CHAPTER III
QUESTIONS ABOUT
VARIOUS PEOPLE

Robert Dabney Questions
QUESTION #1060
What do you think of the Confederate Pastor, Dabney? Personally, I like the old conservative teachings from the south, and I think the south was mostly right.
ANSWER #1060
From the LINK below, I would not agree with Dabney's racial or Calvinist views. I think he stood for the King James Bible. I'm not sure of this. If so, I would agree with that much.
http://en.wikipedia.org/wiki/Robert_Lewis_Dabney

Information About Josephus
QUESTION #1061
Do any of your publications that I might have discuss Josephus other than the brief mention in your text, *"Defending the King James Bible?"* Did he rely on the Septuagint?
ANSWER #1061
I don't have anything else, but http://en.wikipedia.org/wiki/Josephus might be of help to you with more information about Josephus.

A Lesbian on the NIV Committee?
QUESTION #1062
You have stated you have various works on Virginia Mollenkott. Is there one that is considered the definitive work?
ANSWER 1062
I would suggest that you get **BFT #2319, 15 pages @ $3.00 + $2.00 S&H**, *"Lesbian Mollenkott (On NIV Committee) Out of Closet"* by Yvonne Waite & Dr. D. A. Waite. It lays out the facts pretty clearly.

Is Virginia Mollenkott a Lesbian?

QUESTION #1063

I read the statement that the New International Version (NIV) translation committee had at least one lesbian/homosexual person on the team. Is that documented as to who that is?

ANSWER #1063

The lesbian/homosexual person on the NIV committee was Virginia Mollenkott. Here are some articles on Virginia Mollenkott and her lesbianism.

BFT #2490/8, Cassette @ $4.00 + S&H, *"Lesbian Virginia Mollenkott Exposed & Her Part on the NIV"* by Yvonne S. Waite,

BFT #2491, Cassette @ $4.00 + S&H, *"Lesbian Virginia Mollenkott--Her Lesbianism & Part in the NIV"* by Yvonne S. Waite.

BFT #0697, Cassette, @ $4.00 +S&H, *"Interview With Pro-Lesbian Virginia Mollenkott"* by Yvonne S. Waite.

BFT #2319, 15 pages @ $3.00, *"Lesbian Mollenkott (On NIV Committee) Out of Closet"* by Yvonne S. Waite.

BFT #2439, Cassette, @ $4.00, *"Lesbian Mollenkott Interview on NIV Translation & Homosexuality"* By Dr. J. R. Chambers.

BFT #2439-P, 30 pages @ $4.00 + S&H, *"Lesbian Mollenkott Interview on NIV Translation & Homosexuality* By Dr. J. R. Chambers & Yvonne S. Waite.

The various changes in the Greek text of the King James Bible vs. the modern versions number over 8,000. All of them are available in Dr. Jack Moorman's *8,000 Differences between the TR and the Critical Text* (**BFT #3084 @ $20.00 + $8.00 S&H**) Though some are minor differences, 356 have to do with doctrinal passages. These are outlined in almost 200 pages by Dr. Moorman in his book *Early Manuscripts, the Church Fathers, and the King James Version* (**BFT #3230 @ $20.00 + $8.00 S&H**).

Virginia Mollenkott NIV Contributor?

QUESTION #1064

Above is a website that has all of the translators of the New International Version. Virginia Mollenkott is not on that list. However if you Google her name it does say she has been affiliated with various movements of pro-lesbianism. What was the source that whoever arrived at the conclusion that Virginia Mollenkott was in fact one of the translators on the New International Version work?

ANSWER #1064

She was a __language consultant__, but she was on a list called a list of "__TRANSLATORS__" in the first edition that was sent out (which I have). Since her exposure, NIV has taken her name out of everything. They sent her huge "swatches" (her word) of material to go over since she has a Ph.D. in English.

Darwin and Westcott and Hort

QUESTION #1065

When I had attended your King James Bible Seminar, I remembered some quotation from Hort asking Westcott something like this: "*Have you read Darwin, I think you will find him to be quite unanswerable.*" What is the connection between Darwin and Westcott and Hort?

ANSWER #1065

One thing is clear. Charles Darwin was a contemporary with Westcott and Hort. In fact, John Dewey also lived at the same time.

John MacArthur's Greek Text

QUESTION #1066

I was saved under John MacArthur's ministry and I do appreciate the style of preaching he has done. However, I have pointed out on the various forums for Mr. MacArthur's ministry that often times, he questions God's word by saying "*such text is not in the originals*" or other such verses. The people automatically label me a KJV-onlyist which I am. However, I even tell them if he uses any version of the Bible, why does he have to question the text so much? Am I wrong in this line of thinking to believe that someone who claims to have such a high regard for the Bible should not be correcting the Bible by claiming there are portions not in the originals? Thank you for your emails about your King James Bible superiority sermons.

ANSWER #1066

MacArthur believes in an erroneous New Testament Gnostic Critical Greek Text that changes the Received Text of the King James Bible in over 8,000 places. Among these 8,000 places are over 356 doctrinal passages. When you have time, I would suggest you listen to my one-hour PDF fourfold defense of the King James Bible. Write me at BFT@BibleForToday.org and I'll send you this PDF. This will show why MacArthur's Gnostic Critical Greek Text is so erroneous. I would leave that church if they follow such a Greek Text.

Riplinger's "Inspired" Translations
QUESTION #1067

I quote Dr. Waite in a statement he made in response to Gail Riplinger's book *"Traitors,"* saying *"Not a single translation in any language is inspired by God, including the King James Bible and the other Bibles since Acts 2."* Why no inspiration of any Bible translation since Acts 2? Could you please inform me about how I can understand this?

ANSWER #1067

The simple answer to Gail Riplinger's heresy of *"inspired translations"* is the simple fact that there are no *"inspired translations"* in existence, including the King James Bible. Riplinger teaches the heresy that in Acts 2 and beyond they had many *"inspired translations."* Only the original Hebrew, Aramaic, and Greek Words were *"inspired of God"* and *"God-breathed."* For more information about this heresy, go to Chapter VII in this book on *Questions About Bible Inspiration.*

John MacArthur On "Servant"
QUESTION #1068

John MacArthur, in his new book, *Slave*, claims that the word *"servant"* in 1 Corinthians was mistranslated by the early Bible translators, in the Geneva Version and in the King James Bible. He claims that the proper translation should be the word *"slave,"* which appears in the Roman Catholic Bible. I doubt his claim, but, since I do not know any Greek, I thought that an e-mail to you would be in order. If he is wrong, please send me a reply. *"Slave"* is also used in the New King James Bible.

ANSWER #1068

MacArthur's statement is very confusing because it implies that *"slave"* is the **only** word that can be used and that *"servant"* can never appear in the King James Bible. **Only** if the Greek word is DOULOS, can it be translated as *"slave."* It can **never** be translated *"slave"* accurately if the English word, *"servant"* is a translation of the Greek word DIAKONOS which can **never** mean *"slave."*

Book by Edward Hills

QUESTION #1069

What do you think of *The King James Bible Defended* by Edward F. Hills?

ANSWER #1069

Though I disagree with some of his hyper-Calvinist Presbyterian theology, Dr. Hills takes a good stand for the King James Bible and the Greek Textus Receptus and the Hebrew Masoretic Words underlying it. Because of this, we carry this book by him. To get a copy of this book, you can order it as **BFT #84, 280 pages, $18.00 + $8.00 S&H.**

Riplinger's "Replacement" Theology

QUESTION #1070

I listened to your rebuttal of Gail Riplinger. You mentioned *"replacement theology"* as for her *"replacing"* the Hebrew, Aramaic, and Greek Words with the King James Bible. I was reading a *Friends of Israel* magazine and came across *"replacement theology"* articles. I googled the term and came across the Vatican heresy of the Roman Catholic Church replacing Israel as recipient of God's blessing. The Roman Catholic Church calls this *"replacement theology."* When you mentioned *"replacement theology"* in your rebuttal against Gail Riplinger, did you mean the same thing as the Vatican's heresy of *"replacement theology"*?

ANSWER #1070

I didn't have in mind the Roman Catholic Church's definition of *"replacement theology"* when I used the term for what Gail Riplinger has done with the Bible. She has *"replaced"* God's Hebrew, Aramaic, and Greek Words with the English words of the King James Bible. This is a very dangerous and serious *"replacement theology"* heresy which replaces the Words that God gave to us with the words that man translated for us.

Followers of Ruckmanism

QUESTION #1071

Could I impose on you to help me with a long-standing question? Try as I may, I am not able to determine with certainty if the following men are Ruckmanites or not. It doesn't seem that they are, but I certainly could be wrong. I have much material from the Dean Burgon Society (DBS) or the Bible For Today (BFT), but if this question comes up regarding these men who are not DBS men, I would like to give an accurate answer.

Dr. Douglas D. Stauffer
Dr. Sam Gipp
Dr. William Grady
ANSWER #1071

As for these three men as being followers of Peter Ruckman or not, let me say the following:

1.   Dr. Douglas D. Stauffer--I'm not sure whether he is a Ruckman follower or not. He might be. He is definitely a hyper-dispensationalist as Ruckman is, thinking that only Paul's letters are written to us today. He does not think Hebrews (if not by Paul), James, 1 and 2 Peter, 1, 2, and 3 John, Jude, and Revelation are written to us during this age of grace. I strongly disagree with him on this position. He does stand for the King James Bible, but I do not know if he believes it is *"inspired"* in some sense. However, though there are certainly some things I would agree with him about, because of his erroneous and dangerous hyper-dispensationalist view, I would not recommend that he should be followed either in his preaching or in any of his books.

2.   Dr. Samuel Gipp--he is definitely a follower of Peter Ruckman. I understand that he was trained at Peter Ruckman's school. I was also told that he speaks in Ruckman's place when Ruckman is not able to go to various places. On John Ankerberg's television program on the King James Bible, Samuel Gipp was asked a question by one of the men who support the Gnostic Critical Greek Text of the New Testament. He was asked if a Russian wanted to know the Bible, what should he do. Gipp said he would have to learn English and go to the King James Bible. He did not believe any other translation of the Bible was truly God's Word. This is pure Ruckmanism.

3.   Dr. William Grady–he is a total Ruckmanite. He wrote the Foreword to a pro-Ruckman book which I have in my possession. In the Foreword, he shows himself to be a 100% follower of Ruckman's position. In fact, in the Foreword, he wants to be in close association with Peter Ruckman in Heaven. I no longer carry, use, or recommend his books, though I once did before I knew of his Ruckmanite position on the King James Bible.

Samuel Gipp's Teaching
QUESTION #1072

That Pastor from Southampton, England, who has Samuel Gipp come and preach for him, had a barbeque last week and invited many people. He gave out free a book by Samuel Gipp. I really need to know if he said years ago on the John Ankerburg show something like, *"If a Russian person wants to read a Bible, he has to learn English, and read the King James Bible."* If there is something to warn the Christians here in England about, it is this man, I want to do it with the facts which can be accessed. Can you help at all, Pastor?

ANSWER #1072

This quote is from my book o0n *Foes of the King James Bible*, at about pages 7-8. It is **BFT #2777 @ $10.00 + $8.00 S&H**. It is issue #6 of many issues in the John Ankerberg TV series. I quoted directly from the script of the broadcast. Hope this helps. <u>Gipp is a pupil and follower of heretic Peter Ruckman, and though he might have some materials that are helpful, they are based on his false view of the King James Bible.</u>

Must a Russian Learn the English Bible?

#6 Issue: John Ankerberg asked Dr. Gipp: "If a guy is in Russia and he really wants to get to the truth of the Word of God, would he have to learn English?" Dr. Gipp answered: "Yes." (Script, pp. 1-2)

Comment by Dr. Waite:

"This position once again represents serious error. This is the position of Dr. Ruckman and Dr. Gipp and their followers. They believe that the King James Bible in English is the only language that God has preserved, and the only thing that should be used today. Their argument goes something like this: God wrote the Old Testament in one language, Hebrew. He wrote the New Testament in one language, Greek. Today, since English is the predominant language of the world, it is the English King James Bible that should be used. For this reason, Dr. Gipp said that the man in Russia would have to learn English "to get the truth of the Word of God." The implication is that he would have to use the King James Bible rather than an accurate translation into the Russian language. This is a strange answer. Romans 16:26, speaking of the "gospel" which was a hidden mystery in the Old Testament, says:

"But now is made manifest, and by the scriptures of the prophets, according to the commandment of the everlasting God, made known to all nations for the obedience of faith:"

This verse implies that the Scriptures which are "made known to all nations" should be in their own heart language or mother tongue so they can have "the obedience of faith." I believe that God is interested in having His Words translated accurately into the languages of every person in this world. The translation must be taken from the proper Hebrew and Greek texts. The translators must be proficient, professional, and able. The technique of translation must have verbal equivalence and have the forms of the words equivalent wherever possible. The theology must be sound and accurate as well.

God does not restrict His Words and His Truth to the English language. Do you understand the error of Samuel Gipp when he says in order to know "the truth of the Word of God" you have to know English? That is serious heresy and error. We want God's Hebrew and Greek Words translated accurately into every language in the world. Sad to say, this is not presently being done by the United Bible Societies, the American Bible Society, the Wycliffe Translators, or similar groups. These groups use erroneous Bible texts of Hebrew and Greek, erroneous techniques of translation, resulting in erroneous and heretical theology.

Do you remember the Day of Pentecost in Acts Chapter 2? God the Holy Spirit performed a miracle on the 12 apostles that were there. Here the Jews were gathered from every corner of the globe for the feast of Pentecost. They needed the gospel of Christ. There were at least 12 different languages present from all over the then-known world. These Jews had to receive the gospel of our Saviour in their own language. Now, God did not make those people learn the Hebrew, the language of the Old Testament. He did not make them learn Greek, the language of the New Testament. He performed a miracle of languages or tongues. He permitted each one of those 12 apostles to preach and teach in the 12 different languages of the people who were gathered there on that feast day. They preached the gospel in those languages so that the people understood their own languages. God performed that miracle so that the gospel could go out. The people wondered how they heard the gospel in their own language. I think that this illustrates that God wants His Truth in all the languages of the world including those that were gathered on the Day of Pentecost.

When Samuel Gipp says that English is the only way to go and that the English corrects, gives "advanced revelation," and at times even contradicts the Hebrew and Greek, we believe that this is total heresy. God's Word in Hebrew and Greek are the very words that God spoke to the original writers, gave to us through accurate copies, and preserved for us down to the present age. <u>To say that the only word that God has preserved for us is in English and not preserved in Hebrew and Greek and that everyone who wants to know the Word of God must learn English is blatant heresy and perversion of truth.</u>"

I hope this helps you to refute the false teachings of Samuel Gipp there in England or wherever he might go.

Peter Ruckman and Bill Grady

QUESTION #1073

A friend of mine recommended I take a look at a book entitled *Final Authority* by Dr. William Grady. I found something interesting that was said in it and wondered if it is right. Is it true that the 10% of the over 5,000 manuscripts disagree "wildly" with the remaining 90% of the manuscripts? What happened with the 10%? Were there terrible scribal errors?

ANSWER #1073

Bill Grady takes a similar position to that of Peter Ruckman. He believes the King James Bible is somehow "*inspired.*" Because of this, I must part company with him on this point. We formerly carried his book, but no longer do so. The Gnostic Critical Greek manuscripts do not comprise 10% of the manuscript evidence, but less than 1% of the evidence. The Vatican and Sinai manuscripts and about 43 others in Dean Burgon's day is all they have. 45 is not even 1% of the over 5,500 MSS now in existence.

Bill Gothard

QUESTION #1074

I am a church member in Melbourne, Australia. Earlier this year I ordered a book from Bible For Today written by you, named *Bill Gothard's Sex Scandals–Watergate or Waterloo?–An Evaluation of Some of the Primary Documents*, because I was doing research for our church. Our church organized Bill Gothard's Basic Seminar DVD's from IBLP for our members to watch. However there were members questioning Bill's teaching and what he acted like in real life, referring to the sexual scandal. Thus I ordered the book.

After reading the book, I emailed Bill Gothard, asking him some questions. He recently replied. Now I want to seek your opinion on whether Mr. Gothard is telling the truth:

1.   When asked how he regarded your book, Mr. Gothard said:

> "*Many years ago, I pointed out errors in Dr. Waite's writing and asked if he would correct them. He said that he did not have the money to do this, so I sent him a check to cover his expenses. However, he still did not correct what he had written.*"

Is it true? Do you admit the errors in your book?

2.   In your book, you clearly point out that Bill Gothard knew exactly the nature and extent of Steve's sexual fornication. Now Mr. Gothard replied to me, saying:

> "*I want to assure you that when moral misconduct was told to me in 1976, I had no idea that it was as serious as it actually was. Had I known the full story, I would have certainly dealt with matters in a different way.*"

What do you think?

3.   When asked what justified his decision to direct Steve writing the *Character Sketch* books, he replied:

> "*Regarding the character sketch books, I and other researchers wrote all the text in the books. Steve only directed the artist on the nature material.*"

What do you think?

4.   I asked about the confession he made on May 17, 1980, which is included in your book. Mr Gothard said:

> "*The confession that I made was asking forgiveness for not dealing with my brother in a wise and Biblical way. This has also been distorted. I have dedicated my life to working with young people and I love them dearly. It has never been my intention to defraud or deceive. Early in my life I made a vow that I would never kiss a girl before marriage or improperly touch her and God has given the grace to keep this vow.*"

What has been distorted?

5.   When asked about the class actions against IBLP, Mr .Gothard said:

> "*The class actions were initiated by those who wanted to take over the assets of the Institute. The actions were without any merit and were dropped.*"

What's your insight about the class actions?   Did these people who appeared in your book make a fuss over nothing? Are they telling lies?

6.   So far I am getting a bit confused. I hope you can take some time to reply, which will help me (and our church members as well) greatly in discerning the truth from heresy.

ANSWER #1074

Here is a summary of what I think about Bill Gothard. I will follow this with a point for point answer to the questions that have been asked.

My Summary About Bill Gothard

I have not kept up with Gothard currently. (1) He is an ecumenical compromiser regarding the Bible's doctrines. I strongly disagree with this. (2) He is still wrong on many of his views of being single. I strongly disagree with this. (3) He tries to be an expert on medical matters on which he is ignorant. I strongly disagree with this. (4) He tries to be an expert on marriage, never having been married. I strongly disagree with this. (5) His cover-up of his brother Steve's serious sexual sins and lying about it makes me believe he cannot ever be trusted again for anything. I strongly disagree with this. (6) His lying to you about his attempt to change my interview with him still makes me distrust his integrity on any matter. I strongly disagree with him on this.

My Specific Answers To The Six Questions Asked About Bill Gothard

1.   I did not admit there were any errors in my book. I recorded my interview with Gothard and quoted him exactly. He didn't like some of his own answers so he gave money for me to add some things. I reprinted my analysis and added the things he wanted me to add. He also wanted me to subtract some of the things which he had told me. I did not subtract anything. This is all recorded in my **BFT #276**, 43 pages @ $6.00 + $3.00 S&H, *Bill Gothardism–A Critical Evaluation.*

2.   I do not think Gothard would have dealt with his brother's sin because he needed him to write many of his materials. I believe his brother, Steve, continued writing materials for Gothard even after the sin was revealed. Gothard was very reluctant to let his brother leave. If he really condemned his repeated fornication, why didn't he fire him?!! The entire sin of his brother and Gothard's cover-up is detailed in my book *Bill Gothard's Sex Scandals–Watergate Or Waterloo?* (**BFT #1036, 200 page, @ $22.00 + $8.00 S&H**).

3.   From the evidence of the Gothard leaders, it is clear that Steve was so valuable to the material used by Gothard that even though he had committed horrible fornication and/or sodomy on one or more of Gothard's female staff, Bill Gothard secretly brought him back to help without announcing this to the public who would have seen his hypocrisy and insincerity in this action.

4.   I don't know what Gothard thinks has been "*distorted.*" Why didn't he name it and correct it rather than just give his unsupported charge of "*distorted*"? I'm sure I quoted his confession correctly without distortion. I

might have made some comments on it, but that is not distortion of the alleged confession.

5.   These leaders within the Gothard leadership were not wanting his millions of dollars of assets. They just wanted to expose the hypocrisy and wickedness of this professed moral leader. I am glad they told what they knew and brought it out into the light. They had every right to seek to get their salaries that they had been promised by Gothard. I believe they told the truth about this man, even though they were loyal to him for so many years. They had had enough of his hypocrisy and deception.

6.   You are free to follow Gothard wherever he might lead you. As for me and my house, he has forfeited his moral leadership due to his mishandling of his brother's deep and wicked sexual sin. He resigned for a brief while (and should have stayed resigned) only to come back asking people's forgiveness. People still look up to Gothard as a god instead of a devil. They follow him, rather than God's Words in the Bible. His wicked brother finally married and then was so perverted in his sexual life that his wife divorced him.

Do I Agree With Peter Ruckman?
QUESTION #1075
I was in Sunday school when a man in my class said that men like Ruckman and Waite taught that you can only be saved from a King James Bible. Is this true? I have read your material for years and listened to a lot of your audio. I have never heard you say this personally, and I know that you shouldn't have been lumped in with such a false teacher as Peter Ruckman, but I wanted to make sure of your stand on that issue before I went to my brother in Christ and let him know that you do not teach that a person can only be saved from the King James Bible.

ANSWER #1075
Thank you for your note. I do not agree with Peter Ruckman on this or on most of his other positions. Though I stand for the accuracy and reliability of the King James Bible above all other English versions, it is possible for people to be saved while reading other versions. I know some people who have been saved in this way. However, as soon as they are saved, I recommend that they should turn to the King James Bible for growth and accurate knowledge of the Words of God in English. I agree with you that I do not want to be lumped together with Peter Ruckman, Gail Riplinger, or any of their followers. I believe that they are heretics in their views about the King James Bible being "*inspired*" as well as in many other areas. I'm glad you have listened to many of my audio messages. I hope they have been helpful to you.

Lewis Sperry Chafer & the Gospels

QUESTION #1076

I have been working my way through Dr. Lewis Sperry Chafer's *Systematic Theology*. I am reading about his teachings on the two "*gospels*" of the New Testament and I would like your thoughts on this.

ANSWER #1076

The "*gospel of the kingdom*" refers to the good news about when the Lord Jesus Christ will establish His millennial kingdom on this earth. The "*gospel of the grace of God*" is the gospel of personal salvation to those who genuinely believe in and trust the Lord Jesus Christ as their Saviour from sin. If we remember that the word, "*gospel*," means "*good news*," we can use this word in various ways, as the New Testament uses it, without being confused or misunderstood. As one of Dr. Chafer's students from 1948 through 1952, I understand and agree with his views on this subject.

Dr. Chafer and Calvinism

QUESTION #1077

I believe that God **offers** salvation to all people. I also believe that man has the God-given ability either to accept or reject the Gospel of the Lord Jesus Christ when it is presented to him. How do you understand "*elect*"? I have been enjoying Dr. Lewis Sperry Chafer's *Systematic Theology*. He seems to be Calvinistic in his views. I do not agree with this part of his theology.

ANSWER #1077

Yes, Dr. Chafer is Calvinistic in part. I disagree with that part of his Calvinism. As I do, he departs from hyper-Calvinism in his understanding of the atonement of the Lord Jesus Christ. Hyper-Calvinism teaches a "*limited atonement*" which means the Lord Jesus Christ died only for a limited group of people called the "*elect*." Dr. Chafer believed and taught an "*unlimited atonement*" which means the Lord Jesus Christ died for the sins of the whole world, not just for a limited group called the "*elect*."

Regarding the Bible's teaching on "*election*," I believe the easiest way to understand it is to consider it as a "*corporate election*." Just as God chose Israel corporately, or as a body, so God chose the church corporately, or as a body, from all eternity past. The church was chosen and founded as a body or a group. Then, when a person genuinely receives the Lord Jesus Christ as their Saviour, they become members of that previously elect or chosen corporate body, the church. I believe this view of corporate election is both Biblical, understandable, and against the wrong views of the hyper-Calvinists.

John R. Rice and the KJB

QUESTION #1078

I am continuing to do research for our film series and was wondering if you could tell me anything about John Rice, the founder of the *Sword of the Lord*. Is it true that he really thought the Vatican/Sinaitic manuscripts could correct the King James Bible? This interview was near the end of his life. Do you think it fairly represents Mr. Rice? If this is true, perhaps this explains why champions of Rome's critical text such as Cyrus Scofield and Bob Jones Sr. are held in esteem as great men of God by the *Sword of the Lord* ministry to this day.

ANSWER #1078

Regarding John R. Rice's view of the Bible, let me site some passages where he is either totally wrong or unclear as to his position. These are quoted below. I think the interview correctly depicts Rice's position on the Bible. He has waffled all over the place. While claiming to use the King James Bible, he had other preachers in his *Sword of the Lord* paper that used all other kinds of incorrect versions. As many popular **evangelists**, preachers, and editors of Christian papers do, Rice tried to please all men as to the Bible. He wanted to hold the King James Bible people close so he could get their money and influence while at the same time not alienating the new version people who were being taught the new versions from their colleges and seminaries from 1881 and onward.

Rice's Positions And My Answer

1. Answer by John R. Rice:
    *"It has been shown again and again that with every possible variation found in any of the manuscripts, **there is not a single doctrine of the Bible changed, not a single historical event affected, not a single duty commanded that is thus clouded**. God has wonderfully preserved His Scripture."*

This is total error! Dr. Jack Moorman has identified **356 doctrinal passages** where the Gnostic Critical Greek Text is in error in doctrines, historical events, and duties. All 356 of these passages are found in his book,

Early Manuscripts, Church Fathers, and the Authorized Version **(BFT #3230 @ $20.00 + $8.00 S&H)**

2.   Question: "*What is your opinion of the American Standard Version (ASV)?*"

2.   Answer by John R. Rice:

"*The translators of the ASV had the advantage of having access to the three oldest manuscripts with which we are familiar--the Vatican, the Alexandrian, and the Sinaitic manuscripts. It corrects some mistakes in the KJV. One very serious error in the translation of the KJV makes Revelation 22:14 say, 'Blessed are they that do his commandments, that they may have right to the tree of life, and may enter in through the gates into the city.' That would seem to make the plan of salvation by works and that people go to Heaven by keeping God's commandments. But it is not a good translation. The ASV correctly says: 'Blessed are they that wash their robes, that they may have the right to come to the tree of life, and may enter in by the gates into the city. . . .*"

This is no "*advantage*" at all.   Furthermore, the King James Bible translators knew of these false Vatican and Sinai manuscripts from other copies that followed them and they rejected all of them.   Rice wrongly thought these Gnostic Critical Greek Texts were all right when, in fact, they are seriously defective in 356 doctrinal passages, and in many other places as well.   Dr. Jack Moorman has chronicled over 8,000 differences in the Greek New Testament Texts of the Vatican and Sinai manuscripts when compared to the Received Text underlying the King James Bible.   This documentation is found in his book, *8,000 Differences Between The Critical Text and the Textus Receptus* **(BFT #3084 @ $20.00 + $8.00 S&H)**.

3.   Answer by John R. Rice (quite similar to #1 above):

"*There are many, many translations. The differences in the translations are so minor, so insignificant, that we can be sure not a single doctrine, not a single statement of fact, not a single command or exhortation, has been missed in our translations. And where the Word of God is not perfectly translated in one instance, it is corrected in another translation.*"

Once again, this answer is in total error. Differences are not "*minor.*" As Dr. Moorman has detailed in the two books cited above, there are over "*8,000 Differences*" in all. Among these differences, Dr. Moorman has listed 356 "*doctrines, statements of fact, commands, or exhortations*" that "*have been missed*" by use of the Vatican and Sinai Gnostic Critical Greek Texts on which the ASV and other new versions have been based. If the "*other translations*" have the wrong Greek foundation, they cannot "*correct*" anything.

Not An "Everyday Couple"
QUESTION #1079

One of the pastors in Albania said Jesus came into the world "*to an everyday couple.*" Is it doctrinally right to say "*to an everyday couple*"?

ANSWER #1079

I wouldn't call Mary and Joseph "*an everyday couple.*" They were godly Jews specially selected by the Lord. In that sense, they were not "*an everyday couple.*"

CHAPTER IV
QUESTIONS ABOUT
THE KING JAMES BIBLE

The KJB and the Textus Receptus
QUESTION #1080

I sincerely believe that the King James Bible is the best translation. I have spent some time studying this very controversial issue. I would like to know if there is a Bible other than the King James Bible that is based on the Received Text, the Textus Receptus.

ANSWER #1080

Of the current English translations, only the King James Bible is solidly based on the Textus Receptus and carefully translated from it. The New King James Version claims to be based on the Textus Receptus, but I found (just by accident) at least three places where it was translated from the Gnostic Critical Text. Another friend told me that he had found over 100 other places where it was not based on the Textus Receptus. Regardless of how many times the New King James Version departed from the Textus Receptus, my careful research has found that in over 2,000 places, it has inaccurately translated its Greek text. (See **BFT #1442** @ **$12.00 + $8.00 S&H**)

The Cambridge 1769 KJB
QUESTION #1081

I am still confused over the Bible issue. Someone said to me, if you did not have a 1769 Cambridge Bible it, was not an Authorized Version. What do you believe about this?

ANSWER #1081

Though there are many publishers of what they call the "King James Version," I believe that the most accurate wording of the 7th edition of the

King James Bible is in the 1769 Cambridge Bible. Our *Defined King James Bible* was taken from the 1769 Cambridge edition. I have found it to be more accurate in many places than the Oxford edition of the King James Bible.

Is the KJB All We Need?

QUESTION #1082

How would you answer the comment that: "*The King James Bible is all we really need*"?

ANSWER #1082

Though the King James Bible is a true, accurate, and reliable translation of its inerrant, preserved underlying Hebrew, Aramaic, and Greek Words, this statement is a dangerous statement that is not true as it stands. It is a statement that is made repeatedly by Bible heretics Peter Ruckman, Gail Riplinger, and their followers. Since they believe wrongly and falsely that the King James Bible was "*given by inspiration of God*" or "*inspired*" as a new "*revelation*" which supersedes and supplants the original Hebrew, Aramaic, and Greek Words which God gave us, they believe this statement. This is not only untrue, but it is a serious heresy which is believed by many who defend the King James Bible. No one should scuttle or throw out God's original Bible's Hebrew, Aramaic, and Greek Words in favor of any "*translation*" of those Words in any language of the world.

This statement would also make it impossible to have and use accurate translations of the Bible in languages other than English. This is also the belief of Peter Ruckman, Gail Riplinger, and their followers. It is another erroneous and heretical belief.

The 400ᵗʰ Anniversary of the KJB

QUESTION #1083

When was the 400ᵗʰ anniversary of the King James Bible?

ANSWER #1083

The article below shows that the King James Bible was published in the month of May, 1611, 400 years before May of 2011. If this article is correct, the 400ᵗʰ anniversary of the King James Bible was May, 2011.

http://www.kingjamesbibleonline.org/King-James-Bible-Anniversary/

KJB's "Updating" in 2000-2003
QUESTION #1084
Have you heard of the updating of the King James Bible? It was done in 2000-2003. I was just wondering if you have critiqued it.
ANSWER #1084
This so-called "updating" is totally unsatisfactory. For one reason, omits "thee" and "ye" to distinguish the 2nd person singular from the 2nd person plural. For example, In John 3:7, they change the King James Bible's accurate differentiation between the 2nd person singular and 2nd person plural from:

> *"Marvel not that I said unto **thee, Ye** must be born again."*

Was changed to::

> *"Marvel not that I said unto **you, You** must be born again."*

In this translation, there is no distinction between the first *"you"* which is singular (THEE) as in the King James Bible and the Greek text, and *"you"* plural (YE) as in the King James Bible and the Greek text. I would stick to the old King James Bible rather than this "updated" one. Also, in Matthew 3:3:

> *"For this is he that was **spoken of by the prophet Esaias**, saying, The voice of one crying in the wilderness, Prepare ye the way of the Lord, make his paths straight."*

This "updated" King James Bible reads: *"spoken of by the prophet **Isaiah**."* This letter-for-letter (transliteration) must be ESAIAS as in the King James Bible rather than the re-spelling of "ISAIAH." I'm sure they have the same errors in failing to transliterate the names of ELIAS, JEREMY, and others. I recommend that you stay with the old King James Bible as used in our *Defined King James Bible*.

The Cambridge & Oxford KJB's
QUESTION #1085
I have a *Defined King James Bible*--in fact I have four of them and enjoy them very much. I was curious about a couple of things:

(1) What is the difference between the 1611 Edition & the 1769 Cambridge Edition?

(2) Also, I read here awhile back that there was an Oxford Edition. What would be the difference between the 1769 Cambridge Edition and the Oxford Edition.

(3) What version is the *Defined King James Bible* taken from?

ANSWER #1085

1. There are about 1,000 minor changes in spellings between the 1611 and the 1769 King James Bible editions as well as a few different words. I made a comparison of these two editions by listening with my ears to the 1769 Edition and comparing it to the 1611 Edition (**BFT #1294 @ $3.00 + $2.00 S&H**). A later study compared the two editions by using the editor's eyes rather than only his ears. After throwing out some of his changes, I found the total differences to be around 1,000 minor changes.

2. The Oxford King James Bible edition is inferior to the Cambridge King James Bible 1769 edition. It made many changes, though also minor, from the 1611 which it was seeking to duplicate. I have a list of these differences that I can e-mail to those requesting it.

3. Our *Defined King James Bible* was based on the King James Bible Cambridge 1769 Edition.

Roman Catholic Influence on KJB?

QUESTION #1086

I was just watching on you-tube their version of the story of the Bible. Someone said that the King James Bible is a translation which was influenced by Roman Catholics. Among other things, they said the King James translators used the Douay/Rheims Catholic version for their translation. Is this correct?

ANSWER #1086

It is a lie that the King James Bible was influenced by Roman Catholics. To show the opposition that the King James translators had for Roman Catholicism, the Popes of Rome were mentioned in a bad light in five places in their original *Preface To The Reader.*

Easier to Read Than KJB?

QUESTION #1087

I would like to know if there is a modern English version translated from the Textus Receptus that also uses correct translation techniques from an orthodox Christian viewpoint. I enjoy the Authorized Version, but I occasionally am asked about *"easier to read"* translations. Admittedly, there are a few words and phrases in the King James Bible that are difficult for the modern reader to understand. I teach a college-age Sunday school class and have led a Bible study at the University of Louisville. What suggestions do you have? Thank you for your faithful ministry defending God's word.

ANSWER #1087

Though there is one current version in English that is allegedly based on the Textus Receptus (the NKJV), I don't trust the accuracy of its translation technique. I found over 2,000 places where they have either added, subtracted, or changed in some other way the Hebrew, Aramaic, or Greek Words that underlie the King James Bible. For example, John 3:7 and many other places demand the use of "thee" and "ye" to distinguish between the 2nd person ("you") singular and the 2nd person ("you") plural. I recommend our Bible For Today's *Defined King James Bible* where the 600 or so uncommon words are defined accurately in the footnotes.

http://www.biblefortoday.org/kj_bibles.asp is the LINK that tells about this Bible. This is our answer to the *"few words and phrases in the Authorized Version that are difficult for the modern reader."* You might want to get my book, *Defending the King James Bible* (**BFT #1594 @ $12.00 + $7.00 S&H**) to describe both the fourfold superiority of the King James Bible and the fourfold inferiority of the other English Bible versions. Even if you could find enough superbly qualified translators (like those who gave us the King James Bible) to do the translating (which would be next to impossible), it would be very difficult to find a publisher to publish such a Bible. Most of the current publishers will only publish books that use the modern Bible versions rather than the King James Bible. These publishers would probably frown on a Bible that used the Hebrew, Aramaic, and Greek Words underlying the King James Bible since they are not used by the modern Bible versions.

KJB the Source of the Greek NT?

QUESTION #1088

Are you familiar with a King James Bible man named Will Kinney? He has his own web site with many articles. He also has conducted debates with modern version people. He criticizes the Trinitarian Bible Society's Greek text as follows:

> *"Then they defend what they call the 'traditional text' and what they mean by this is the particular variety of Textus Receptus that CAME FROM* [his caps] *the King James Bible. Their 1894 Scrivener edition of the Textus Receptus was a **back-translation** from the KJB into a Greek New Testament Text."*

What do you say?

ANSWER #1088

I do not know much about Will Kinney. On the Internet, one of his articles claims he believes that the King James Bible is *"inspired."* I believe this is heresy. Only the Hebrew, Aramaic, and Greek Words of the Bible are *"inspired."* No translation, including the King James Bible, has been *"inspired"* by God.

Kinney's statement that   the 1894 Scrivener edition of the Textus Receptus was a *"**back-translation**"* from the King James Bible into a Greek New Testament text is also a false and heretical position. This false position is also held by Gail Riplinger, James Price, Michael Sproul, and many others. As a matter of fact, Dr. Frederick Scrivener states, in the Preface of his book, that his Greek text came, with very few exceptions, from Beza's 5th edition Greek text of 1598. He did not *"**back-translate**"* these Greek words from the English King James Bible into Greek as Kinney and these others have falsely claimed. There is not a syllable of proof that this took place.

The Trinitarian Bible Society published Dr. Scrivener's Greek New Testament text. We of the Bible For Today and the Dean Burgon Society have published a photographic reproduction of Scrivener's book. The Greek text is a larger type. It also contains Scrivener's Preface, footnotes, and comments. You can order it as *Scrivener's Annotated Greek Text* (BFT #1670 @ $35.00 + $8.00 S&H).

Is the KJB Trustworthy?

QUESTION #1089

A friend of mine at our church challenged me on the trustworthiness of the King James Bible by stating that it could not be trustworthy because of all the errors the scribes had made. I told him that I was talking about the inerrancy of the Words in Hebrew, Aramaic, and Greek as received by the inspiration of God and faithfully translated down through the ages through the church and best represented by the King James Bible. He thinks I am being naive to think that there could be a trustworthy translation. How would you best answer him?

ANSWER #1089

I would stick to your original statement that the Hebrew, Aramaic, and Greek Words underlying the King James Bible are plenarily and verbally inspired originally and have been preserved, inerrant, infallible, perfect, and pure. I do not like to use any of these five terms for any translation, including the King James Bible. The King James Bible is the only accurate, faithful, reliable, and true translation of God's original preserved Hebrew, Aramaic, and Greek Words. Remember, the Authorized Version of 1611 contained the

Apocrypha with all its errors of which none of these five terms could rightly be used. <u>Also remember that there were at least seven revisions of the King James Bible, including 100's of changes and differences in them.</u> That being the case, I think we should reserve these five terms for God's own Words rather than any translation of those Words. Our King James Bible certainly is trustworthy!

Was the KJB Influenced by Latin?
QUESTION #1090
Is the following statement true?

> *"The Rhemish Bible, like Wycliffe's, lies properly outside the line of English Bibles, because it is a secondary translation based upon the Vulgate. But it is nevertheless of considerable importance in the internal history of the authorised text, for it furnished a large proportion of the Latin words which King James' revisers adopted; and it is to this rather than to Coverdale's Testaments that we owe the final and most powerful action of the Vulgate upon our present Version."*

If it is not true, what proof is there to disprove it?

ANSWER #1090
While it is true that Wycliffe's translation was based on the Latin Vulgate, the King James Bible was not based on Wycliffe's English. It was based upon Beza's 5th edition 1598 Greek Text. Where the foundation words were the same, Wycliffe was consulted along with the other earlier English versions that were based on the Greek text rather than Latin, including the Coverdale Bible, the Matthews Bible, the Great Bible, the Taverner Bible, the Geneva Bible, and the Bishops' Bible. It is totally false to imply, as many have, that our King James Bible was, to any material extent, influenced by any Latin texts or Bible versions.

Was King James a Murderer?
QUESTION #1091
I have always been taught that the 1611 King James Bible was the only true Bible in English. I am just now learning that some have said that King James was a murderer, a pedofile, and a Mason. Is this true? If this is true, how can I know for sure that this person has not manipulated doctrine? I am very disheartened. Please answer.

ANSWER #1091

Let me answer your question in a few separate parts:

1. You have been taught correctly. The King James Bible is the only faithfully translated English Bible in print today.

2. I have no evidence that King James was a murderer.

3. I have no evidence that King James was a pedophile.

4. I have no evidence that King James was a Mason.

5. It is true that King James did many wrong and evil things to those with whom he disagreed. He was by no means a perfect man or a perfect King. But, regardless of whether or not these specific charges against King James are true or false, he was not one of the translators of the King James Bible. He merely "authorized" this translation. There were over 50 skilled translators who translated the King James Bible in an excellent and reliable manner from the original and preserved Hebrew, Aramaic, and Greek Words. Don't throw that Bible away because of alleged and questionable rumors about the King who only "authorized" it but did not translate it.

Is the KJB's Text Inferior?

QUESTION #1092

I have posted an article about the English Standard Version (ESV) on my website. A man by the name of Alan from Australia, read this article and is upset about it. Could you help me to reply to this issue especially to the statement *"The King James Bible is based on an inferior text, the Textus Receptus"*? Your help is very much appreciated.

ANSWER #1092

I would be glad to help you with this doubter. It is clear to me that he is not a learner searching for truth, but, in fact, he is a teacher teaching untruth. I wouldn't waste your time on him. I would treat him as the Lord treated the doubting Pharisees in Matthew 15:12-14 where the Lord said:

> *"Then came his disciples, and said unto him, Knowest thou that the Pharisees were offended, after they heard this saying? But he answered and said, Every plant, which my heavenly Father hath not planted, shall be rooted up. **Let them alone: they be blind leaders of the blind. And if the blind lead the blind, both shall fall into the ditch**."*

"Let them alone" (v. 14.) This man is dead wrong. The opposite is true. The Textus Receptus Words underlying the King James Bible are correct. His Gnostic Critical Greek text underlying the NASV, NIV, ESV and most other

modern translations differ from the Received Greek Words underlying the King James Bible in over 8,000 places. These places are spelled out in Dr. Jack Moorman's book, *8,000 Differences Between the TR and The Critical Text* (**BFT #3084** @ **$20.00 + $8.00 S&H**). In these 8,000 differences Dr. Moorman spells out a total of over 356 doctrinal passages that are affected adversely. Almost 200 pages of details on these 356 doctrinal passages are set forth in Dr. Moorman's book, *Early Manuscripts, Church Fathers and the Authorized Version* (**BFT #3230** @ **$20.00 + $8.00 S&H**). If this man really wants to learn, that's one thing. It seems that he wants to teach his errors. As the Lord Jesus Christ told his disciples about the Pharisees, since he is a *"blind leader of the blind,"* you should just *"let him alone."*

What's Wrong With "KJV Only"?

QUESTION #1093

I wasn't aware that Dr. D. A. Waite was *"KJV-only."* Is this true?

ANSWER #1093

You were wrongly informed. I am not what most people call *"KJV-only."* It depends on how you define *"KJV-only."* I **only** preach, read, and memorize verses from the King James Bible and defend it as the **only** accurate and reliable English translation. I strongly refute Peter Ruckman, Gail Riplinger and their followers who are literally *"King James Version ONLY,"* that is, without need for the underlying Hebrew, Aramaic, and Greek Words. To the Riplinger/Ruckman gang, the following errors are true:

1.   **Error #1**: These false teachers want us to do away with (and never use or consult at any time) the Hebrew, Aramaic, and Greek Words underlying our King James Bible and use **only** the King James Bible English translation.

2.   **Error #2**: These false teachers believe the King James Bible was *"given by inspiration of God"* and *"inspired"* and thus it supplants the only Words that were *"God-breathed"* and *"inspired,"* that is, the Hebrew, Aramaic, and Greek Words that God gave when He gave us the Old and New Testaments.

I do not stand *"only"* for the King James Bible. I also stand for the Hebrew, Aramaic, and Greek Words that underlie it. Because of this, I cannot truly be labeled *"KJV-only."*

The KJB Was Not "Inspired"

QUESTION #1094

When I lived near Boston, Massachusetts, I would listen to Perry F. Rockwood. He died in January, 2008, just before his 91st birthday. I read an article by Perry Rockwood about Dr. Waite on the King James Bible that was not a favorable one, finding fault. I believe Perry F. Rockwood was wrong with the comment, yet he claims that Dr. Waite was wrong.

ANSWER #1094

The disagreement that Perry Rockwood had with me is this: He believed that the King James Bible was *"inspired of God,"* *"inspired,"* and *"God-breathed."* I believe this is a heretical position. The King James Bible is the only true, reliable, and accurate English translation, but those words and phrases should not be used about it. This is the official position of both our Dean Burgon Society and the Bible For Today ministries. Only the Hebrew, Aramaic, and Greek Words underlying the King James Bible are preserved, *"inspired of God, inspired, and God-breathed."* The King James Bible is a **translation** of those "inspired Words" but was not itself *"inspired by God."* This is a very serious heresy that is believed by many of those who are defending the King James Bible. I hope the reader is not one of these people.

KJB Right or Wrong (Rev. 22:14)?

QUESTION #1095

John R. Rice calls the King James Bible translation *"they that do his commandments"* in Revelation 22.14 an *"unfortunate translation."*

Revelation 22:14

*"Blessed are **they that do his commandments**, that they may have right to the tree of life, and may enter in through the gates into the city."*

Then John Rice said that the American Standard Version has it correct when they translate this phrase, *"they that wash their robes."* (1) Do you have any studies on this alleged *"unfortunate translation"*? (2) What New Testament Greek edition should we use and rely upon?

ANSWER #1095

1.   The manuscript evidence for the correct King James Bible reading of *"they that do his commandments"* in Revelation 22:14 is found on page 311 of Dr. Jack Moorman's book, *Early Manuscripts, Church Fathers, and the Authorized Version* (**BFT #3230 @ $20.00 + $8.00 S&H**) if you want to get a copy to check it out.

2.   I believe that the New Testament Greek edition that we should *"use and rely upon"* is the Textus Receptus or Traditional Text edited by Dr. Frederick Scrivener which relied almost exclusively on Beza's 5th edition of 1598. It can be purchased in two different formats: (1) a smaller printed edition without Scrivener's notes is **BFT #471 @ $14.00 + $7.00 S&H** or (2) a larger

printed edition with Scrivener's notes with annotations where the Critical Text changes the Greek Words on each page is **BFT #1670 @ $35.00 + $8.00 S&H**.

The American Standard Version, as the New American Standard Version, the New International Version, the English Standard Version, the Revised Standard Version, the New Revised Standard Version, the New English Version, and 99% of the other modern versions, rely upon the Gnostic Critical Greek Text in the New Testament. This text differs from the Textus Receptus, not only in Revelation 22:14, but also in a total of 8,000 places in all. These differences are found in Dr. Jack Moorman's book, *8,000 Differences Between the Critical Text and the Textus Receptus* (**BFT #1670 @ $35.00 + $8.00 S&H**). Among these "*8,000 differences*" there are 356 doctrinal passages that are affected adversely. All 356 are delineated in Dr. Jack Moorman's book, *Early Manuscripts, Church Fathers, and the Authorized Version* (BFT #3230 @ $20.00 + $8.00 S&H).

Sending the KJB to Others
QUESTION #1096
I have a copy of the King James Bible and am thinking of sending one to the prime minister of Albania, as a gift to commemorate the 400th anniversary of the King James Bible. Do you think that would be a good idea?
ANSWER #1096
That would be a good idea, regardless of how he might use it. It is truth and is able to bring eternal life to him if he reads it carefully and genuinely trust the Lord Jesus Christ as His Saviour.

Is the KJB "Defunct"?
QUESTION #1097
I have been getting quite the kick back from Christian circles out west of the Mississippi who are declaring the King James Bible **defunct** based on its adherence to the "Yahwist" text. They proclaim "Yahweh" was a murderer, therefore the *Concordat Bible* ought to be observed as it holds to the "Elohist" text. Do you have anything on this?
ANSWER #1097
The LINK below has some information on this, though the issue is not clearly presented in it.

http://forum.davidicke.com/showthread.php?t=14182

The King James Bible is based on a true Traditional Masoretic Hebrew Text. Its "*text*" should be questioned. It is a proper Old Testament Text. It is not "*defunct*," nor should it be called "*defunct*." It is the closest and only accurate English translation of the Hebrew, Aramaic, and Greek Words that underlie it. Our God, both in the Old Testament and in the New Testament cannot and should not rightly be called a "*murderer*." That is blasphemy!

Is the KJB All We Need?

QUESTION #1098

A pastor said we have the King James Bible because God said He would "*preserve His Words*." We don't have to know Greek or Hebrew because we have the Bible in English! Is this true?

ANSWER #1098

In the first place, God's promise to "*preserve His Words*" does not refer to the King James Bible or to any other Bible translation. It refers exclusively to God's own original Hebrew, Aramaic, and Greek Words. Because of this, we must never throw away the Hebrew, Aramaic, and Greek Words that underlie the King James Bible. They are the source of the Bible from God Himself. The King James Bible is an accurate, true, and reliable English **translation** from the very Words that God Himself revealed to mankind, but it is not the original Words themselves. These original Words can and should be consulted for further information and meaning, as needed or required. Gail Riplinger and her followers whose position is to throw out and reject these original Hebrew, Aramaic, and Greek Words as being useless and unnecessary since they believe that the King James Bible was "*given by inspiration of God*" and has replaced these original Words.

Why Is the KJB Attacked?

QUESTION #1099

In your opinion, why is the King James Bible thought of as being so dangerous and thus, attacked?

ANSWER #1099

There are a number of reasons for the many attacks on the King James Bible.

1.   **Making money on new versions**. I believe that part of the reason is the desire for publishers to make money on the printing of their new Bible versions.

2.   **Believing in a false Greek text**. Another part of the reason is the belief in the lies of Bishop Westcott and Professor Hort in the formulation of their 1881 false Gnostic Critical Greek text. The facts show this text to be the worst text that ever saw the light of day. And yet the strong belief in the lie that

it is superior rather than inferior has disrupted belief in the superior Traditional Received Greek Text that underlies the King James Bible.

3.   **Uncommon words**. Another part of the attack on the King James Bible is their charge that it contains many uncommon words used in a different sense today. To have people understand the various uncommon words, our Bible For Today has published the *Defined King James Bible* (**BFT #3000 @ $15.00 or $35.00 or $40.00--depending on the binding + $8.00 S&H**).

4.   **Lack of readability**. To show that the King James Bible is as readable or more readable based on the current standards of readability, D. A. Waite, Jr. has written The *Readability of the Authorized Version* (**BFT #2671 @ $7.00 + $4.00 S&H**). This documentation, based on current standards of readability, showed that the King James Bible was either equally readable as the six other English versions examined, or was slightly more readable.

There are no doubt many other reasons for the attacks on the King James Bible, but these are just a few that have been raised.

Websites Standing for the KJB

QUESTION #1100

Can we exchange links between our websites? We share a "*conviction about the reliability of the King James Bible*" and a desire that the truth of God should be faithfully taught.

ANSWER #1100

I am glad you have a "*conviction about the reliability of the King James Bible*." In order for us to link to your site, we would have to know your complete doctrinal statement. Especially we would need your statement on the Hebrew, Aramaic, and Greek Words that underlie the King James Bible. Do you hold those Words as inspired, inerrant, and infallible? What is your view of the King James Bible? Do you believe it was "*inspired of God*," "*inspired*," or "*God-breathed*"? Do you side with Peter Ruckman, Gail Riplinger, and their followers in this view? Do you believe the King James Bible replaces the Hebrew, Aramaic, and Greek Words that underlie it? When you send me your complete doctrinal statement about other doctrines as well, I can make up my mind on your request. Thank you for your interest in our BibleForToday.org website and ministries.

Is the KJB the Word of God?

QUESTION #1101

Why do you say you believe the King James Bible is the Word of God when what you really mean is you believe the Hebrew, Aramaic, and Greek Words from which it comes are the Words of God?

ANSWER #1101

God gave us His Words in Hebrew, Aramaic, and Greek. I believe the King James Bible is the only true, accurate, and reliable English translation of those original, preserved, inspired, inerrant, and infallible Words. In my book, *Defending the King James Bible* (**BFT #1594 @ $12.00 + $8.00 S&H**) I call the King James Bible "*God's Words Kept Intact in English.*" I believe this is the accurate description of what I believe about the King James Bible. It might be called "*the Word of God in English,*" meaning that it is the accurate translation of the proper original language Words in English. However, we should never throw away the Hebrew, Aramaic, and Greek Words from which the King James Bible was translated as do Gail Riplinger, Peter Ruckman, and their followers.

"Castaway" in the KJB

QUESTION #1102

In Mount Calvary Baptist Church's pamphlet "*Trusted Voices on Translation*" Mark Minnick quoted with approval hymn writer Francis Ridley Havergal as stating that "*castaway*" is a wrong translation in 1 Corinthians 9:27 in the King James Bible. She said it should be "*not approved.*" Please comment on this.

ANSWER #1102

"*Castaway*" is one of the various meanings of the Greek word, ADOKIMOS. It is true that literally, it is "*not approved,*" but once the Lord "*disapproves*" your ministry, you might become a "*castaway*" because of it. This is what the King James Bible translators wanted to convey and therefore translated correctly in this way. Both Mark Minnick and Francis Havergal are incorrect in questioning the King James Bible's translation of "*castaway*" in 1 Corinthians 9:27.

Source of KJB Is Not Latin
QUESTION #1103

I have assumed that the King James Bible's New Testament came from the Textus Receptus. Isn't the Textus Receptus a translation into Greek from the Latin Vulgate? What do you mean "*readings*" of the Vatican or the Sinai manuscripts?

ANSWER #1103

All of the King James Bible readings come from the Textus Receptus Traditional Greek Text. The readings do not come from the Latin Vulgate. This version quite often uses readings from the Gnostic Critical Greek Text. This Greek Text differs from that of the Textus Receptus underlying the King James Bible in more than 8,000 places (See Dr. Moorman's book *8,000 Differences Between the Critical Text and the Textus Receptus* (BFT #3084 @ $20.00 + $8.00). "*Readings*" are those words found in either the Aleph (Sinai) or "B" (Vatican) manuscripts (or found in other manuscripts).

Meaning of King James Only
QUESTION #1104

Perhaps you can help me with a term that often comes up. The term that is somewhat confusing is: "*We are only KJV, not KJV only.*" All those whom I heard use the King James Bible exclusively for Sunday school, worship services, and memorization. What is meant by this?

ANSWER #1104

Technically, literally, and usually, those people who believe in "*King James Only (KJVO)*" trust, value, and use **only** the King James Bible. That means they do not use any other translation in any language of the world, only the King James Bible in English. That also means they do not use or refer to God's inerrant, preserved Hebrew, Aramaic, and Greek Words that underlie the King James Bible. Usually, those who say "*we are only KJV,*" they mean that they use (as you have stated in your question) only the King James Bible in their preaching, Sunday School classes, memorization, and in other areas of their church. They do not use any other English version in their church. They also stand for and consult, as needed, the Hebrew, Aramaic, and Greek Words that underlie the King James Bible. I believe these are the main distinctions in the use of these two terms.

King James Bible Terminology

QUESTION #1105

I have three questions I would like you to answer for me if possible.

1. What is the difference between the Authorized Version (AV) and the King James Version (KJV) designations? Some authors use the terms interchangeably but do not explain the distinction.

2. Granting that there might be a few problems with the English King James Bible in translating from the Greek Textus Receptus (GTR), could there also be errors with the GTR?

3. Why can various publishers change some words in their King James Bibles now that it is in the public domain?

ANSWER #1105

1.   The Authorized Version (AV) leaves out King James who turns off some people. King James Bible includes the King. I prefer King James Bible rather than King James Version since it is more than a "version." It is a Bible.

2.   I believe that the Hebrew, Aramaic, and Greek Words underlying the King James Bible are inerrant and perfect since I believe they are the preserved Words that God gave humanity. They are the very Words God gave to mankind.

3.   You are correct. In the USA, there is no copyright on the KJB as there is in England. Because of this, publishers are able to change any words they wish and still call it the King James Bible. We use the Cambridge King James Bible which is faithful to the final revision of the King James Bible in 1769 and is accurate.

CHAPTER V
QUESTIONS ABOUT
BIBLE VERSIONS

Jeremiah 5:10--NASV Vs. The KJB
QUESTION #1106

Perhaps you remember my telling you that I am in an in-depth study with a small group of women, doing the Book of Jeremiah. The study uses the NASB but I use my King James Bible. There has been some opportunity to begin enlightening a few of them about the textual issue. I'm hoping for more opportunity to do so. I've been comparing the King James Bible with the NASB as I go. There seems to be an awfully lot of changes that are made in the Old Testament, too. In checking things, I've found that Strong's is influenced by the LXX, Vulgate, and also Chaldee (whatever that is?). The following is an example:

Jeremiah 5:10--King James Bible

*"Go ye up upon **her walls**, and destroy; but make not a full end: take away **her battlements**; for they are not the LORD'S."*

Jeremiah 5:10--New American Standard Version

*"Go up through **her vine rows** and destroy, But do not execute a complete destruction; Strip away **her branches**, For they are not the LORD'S."*

What is the proper meaning of these words?

ANSWER #1106

The answer to this question is very complicated. I would just like to offer some of the proper meanings of the Hebrew words involved for the reader to examine and come to their proper conclusion. I believe the King James Bible has rendered these terms correctly and the New American Standard Version has rendered these words inaccurately.

"The **WALL**"

08284 sharah {shaw-raw'}
probably from 07791; TWOT - 2355b; n f
AV - wall 1; 1
1) wall
2) (CLBL) vine-row I don't know what this source is, but don't trust it.
     This is used only once in the O. T. Hebrew, probably comes from:
07791 shuwr {shoor}
from 07788; TWOT - 2355b; n m
AV - wall 4; 4
1) wall
     This is used 4 times. <u>The King James Bible editors had it right from the</u> <u>Hebrew.</u>
The **BATTLEMENTS**:
05203 natash {naw-tash'}
a primitive root; TWOT - 1357; v
AV - forsake 15, leave 12, spread 3, spread abroad 1, drawn 1, fall 1, joined
1, lie 1, loosed 1, cast off 1, misc 3; 40
1) to leave, permit, forsake, cast off or away, reject, suffer, join,
    spread out or abroad, be loosed, cease, abandon, quit, hang loose,
    cast down, make a raid, lie fallow, let fall, forgo, draw
    1a) (Qal)
       1a1) to leave, let alone, lie fallow, entrust to
       1a2) to forsake, abandon
       1a3) to permit
    1b) (Niphal)
       1b1) to be forsaken
       1b2) to be loosened, be loose
       1b3) to be let go, spread abroad
    1c) (Pual) to be abandoned, be deserted

I see no meaning for BRANCHES. "Spread abroad" could be like "battlements" or "branches" "entrust to" could give the sense of "battlements."

     The *Oxford English Dictionary* OED) gives this definition of "**battlements**":

"battlement," n. Forms: 4-5 batelment, 5 -eillement, 5-6 -ilment, -illement, -ylment(e, battilment, 6- battlement.

[ME. bateill-, batayle-, batelment, a. OF. *bataille-, *bateillement. f. batailler (= Pr. batalhar). OF. had also (later) batillement, f. ba(s)tillier, whence Caxton's batillement: as to the relation of the two forms see battle v.2]

An indented parapet at the top of a wall, at first used only in fortified buildings for purposes of defence against assailants, but afterwards in the architectural decoration of ecclesiastical and other edifices. The raised parts are called cops or merlons, the indentations embrasures or crenelles."

It could be just decorations on the top of the wall.

The Newberry Bible

QUESTION #1107

Would you recommend the Newberry Wide Margin Study Bible (King James Bible)? I was told that it uses

"a unique system of symbols and signs. Thomas Newberry brings the original Hebrew and Greek text to life on every page."

But from what I understand, he uses the Codex Sinaiticus for the New Testament. Is this true? If so, this "study" Bible is not proper.

ANSWER #1107

As for the *Newberry Study Bible*, I would be very cautious of it and could not recommend it. Here is a quote from *Wikipedia*:

The Englishman's Bible

*"Newberry is most famous for his study Bible. In 1863, he was given a copy of Tischendorf's transcription of the New Testament according to the Codex Sinaiticus[3], in which he made copious handwritten notes, and two years later commenced work on The Englishman's Study Bible, later more commonly known as the Newberry Study Bible. The finished work, with its unique use of signs and symbols to aid understanding of the tenses, and alternative translations, was **much admired by** the likes of William Kelly, **F. F. Bruce** and C. H. Raven."*

The Sinai manuscript is a Gnostic, Critical Text manuscript as you know. If F. F. Bruce (a worshipper of the Gnostic Critical Greek Text) *"admires"* it, it must not be sound and based on the Traditional Greek Text.

The Concordant New Testament
QUESTION #1108
I have an acquaintance that uses the Concordant Literal New Testament. I for one do enjoy the King James Bible and trust it as the preserved Word of God in English. What is your opinion of the Concordant Literal New Testament?
ANSWER #1108
From Wikipedia, here is a brief comment about this New Testament:

> "*A. E. Knoch designed the Concordant Version in such a way as **to put the English reader who lacks a formal knowledge of Koine Greek in possession of all the vital facts of the most ancient codices: Codex Vaticanus, Codex Sinaiticus, and Codex Alexandrinus**. The CPC's efforts yielded a restored Greek text, titled The Concordant Greek Text, containing all of the important variant readings found in the codices mentioned above. This was done with the intent of conforming, as far as possible, to the original autograph manuscripts. An utterly consistent hyper-literal sub-linear based upon a standard English equivalent for each Greek element is to be found beneath each Greek word.*"

As you can see from the above quote, this New Testament exalts the Gnostic Critical Greek Text as represented in *"Codex Vaticanus, Codex Sinaiticus, and Codex Alexandrinus"* and is therefore not to be trusted. http://www.1john57.com/literalerror.htm tells more about the contradictions.

The Peshitta Translation
QUESTION #1109
Was the "Peshitta Bible" originally written in Aramaic or in Greek?
ANSWER #1109
Here is a quote from the *Wikipedia* about the "Peshitta Bible" and the language in which it was written:

> "*The name 'Peshitta' is derived from the Syriac mappaqtâ pšît.tâ (Peshitta), literally meaning 'simple version'. However, it is also possible to translate pšît.tâ as 'common' (that is, for all people), or 'straight', as well as the usual translation as 'simple'. **Syriac is a dialect, or group of dialects, of Eastern Aramaic**, originating in and around Assuristan (Persian ruled Assyria). It is*

written in the Syriac alphabet, and is transliterated into the Latin script in a number of ways: Peshitta, Peshittâ, Pshitta, Pšittâ, Pshitto, Fshitto. All of these are acceptable, but 'Peshitta' is the most conventional spelling in English."

From this quote, you can see the Peshitta was written in Syriac which was a dialect of "*__Eastern Aramaic__*." It was not written in Greek. It is believed that the Peshitta witnesses quite often for the Traditional Text.

Some Foreign Bible Versions

QUESTION #1110

I am trying to determine which foreign language Bibles out there for sale are based on the Textus Receptus for the following languages. Any assistance in identifying good translations in these languages and also suggestions on who might sell these would be appreciated.

FRENCH
PORTUGUESE
VIETNAMESE

ANSWER #1110

I do not have information on sound Vietnamese Bibles. There is a sound French New Testament that has been made in its first draft. It has been made by Pastor Mario Monette and his team in Canada. It should be coming out in a final edition soon. The Trinitarian Bible Society (TBS) in England has published a Portuguese Bible which, though it still has some flaws, is better than the normal Portuguese Bibles.

The New King James Version

QUESTION #1111

What information do you have on the New King James Version (NKJV) that would counter the argument that the NKJV is a more accurate version of the King James Bible. Many pastors out here are using this argument to dissuade the people. Thanks for all the help, I appreciate it greatly.

ANSWER #1111

The most complete analysis of the New King James Version (NKJV) that I have seen is my own **BFT #1442 @ $10.00 + $8.00 S&H**. In this, I have listed over 2,000 specific examples of the NKJV's either adding, subtracting, or changing in some other way the accurate translation of the Hebrew, Aramaic, or Greek Words preserved for us that underlie the King James Bible. Though there are many, many more examples of adding, subtracting, or changing in some other way found in the New American Standard Version or the New International Version, the over 2,000 examples in the New King James Version makes it necessary to abandon the New King James Version and remain with the King James Bible.

Bible Translations
QUESTION #1112

Thank you for the good comments, observations, and clarifications. I was wondering about the statement made in an article that:

> *"The Geneva Bible was **the first Bible to be completely translated to English from the original language**."*

Were the following not counted as being among the first Bibles to be completely translated to English from the original languages: Wycliffe. Tyndale, Coverdale, Matthews, Great Bible, etc.? Did these not precede the Geneva Bible mentioned by the author in his article?

ANSWER #1112

Thanks for clarifying your question. I agree with you that this statement in this article was in error. From my book, *Defending the King James Bible*, p. 198) we notice the following: Though Wycliffe was not *"from the original language"* but from the Latin, the following all preceded the Geneva 1560 Bible translation: (1) Purvey (1388); (2) Nicholas de Hereford (1390); (3) Coverdale (1535); (4) Matthews (1537); (5) James Nycolson (1537); (6) the Great Bible (1539); (7) and Taverner (1539); (8) two anonymous Bibles 1549; (9) and Jugge (1553). As I said before, all of these preceded the Geneva Bible of 1560.

The Freer Logion
QUESTION #1113

I have been reading some articles about the *"freer logion"* on line. Has anyone from your organization considered the possibility that the *"freer logion"* could be a genuine part of Scripture that was removed by "heretics" or by sloppy scribes? I am leaning toward believing that the "freer logion" is Scripturally genuine.

ANSWER #1113

I do not believe this *"freer logion"* that changes Mark 16 should be accepted as genuine. From the Internet sources I have read, it appears to be a forgery. I would not be taken in by any addition to Mark 16 which is not in the Traditional Greek Words underlying our King James Bible.

Problems With the NKJV
QUESTION #1114
I consulted the appendix in the *Defined King James Bible* that you put out for some reference material on the New King James Version (NKJV). It is my understanding that with the exception of the 1967/1977 Stuttgart Hebrew edition, the NKJV used exactly the same underlying texts as the King James Bible (the Old Masoretic and Textus Receptus). While some of the translators may have overlapped from the New International Version (NIV), I've yet to come across documented proof that a Critical text or dynamic equivalence support was manifested by any of the NKJV translators. Could you direct me to any that you might be aware of? I am amazed at the false accusations rendered against the NKJV.

ANSWER #1114
Though the NKJV generally followed the Textus Receptus in the New Testament, I found three places by accident where they did not. A friend of mine found over 100 other places. By my own exhaustive study of the New King James Version from Genesis through Revelation, I found over 2,000 examples of the translators' use of dynamic equivalence, that is, adding to, subtracting from, or changing in some other ways the underlying Hebrew, Aramaic, or Greek Words. This is a serious defect in the New King James Version. If you want to examine these over 2,000 examples, you can get my *Analysis of the New King James Version* (**BFT #1442 @ $10.00 + $8.00 S&H**). In my study, I do not make any "*false accusations*" as you have implied that others do when opposing the New King James Version.

Reese Chronological Bible
QUESTION #1115
I ran across this *Reese Chronological Bible* that someone gave me. I have red flags about it. I would appreciate any insight you may have on this. The Author seems a little questionable. Also, it has these symbols on it and I can't find them in my research efforts. Have you ever seen them or can you point me in the right direction?

ANSWER #1115
Reese made this up many years ago and has been republishing it from time to time ever since. He sent me a copy of it when he first published it. I don't know where my copy is presently. Though his calculations of dates might be right, they also might be wrong, since there are no dates in our Bibles or in the Bible books of either the Old Testament of the New Testament. In other

words, his dates are speculative and though possible, they are not God-given, but man-made.

The order of the books as they appear in of both the Old Testament and New Testament is good enough for me. To sandwich words together from one Bible book and put them into another Bible book perhaps is even sacrilegious. If he called his book *"Guesswork on the Chronology of Bible Verses,"* rather than calling it a *"Bible,"* perhaps it might have some value. Otherwise, I prefer to stick to the Old and New Testament books as God wrote them and in the order He wrote them from the Hebrew, Aramaic, and Greek Words and as translated accurately in our King James Bible.

Other English Versions
QUESTION #1116

If before 1611 there were other Bibles, why did they need the King James Bible? What was wrong with the other English translations?

ANSWER #1116

As one of the key King James Bible translators, John Reynolds, said, in effect, to King James in 1604:

> *"May your majesty be pleased that a new translation be made, **those extant not answering to the originals**."*

Though many of the previous Bibles were founded on the proper Hebrew, Aramaic, and Greek Words the same as the King James Bible, these previous Bibles were not as close as they should be to the Hebrew, Aramaic, and Greek *"originals."* Because they were not as accurate as they should have been, the King James Bible translators were "authorized" to prepare a new Bible which would *"answer to the originals"* accurately and specifically.

Geneva Bible
QUESTION #1117

Recently, websites like *"American Vision," "Patriot,"* Gary Demars, and others, have been pushing, rather vigorously the sale of the "Geneva Bible." They say that it's the Bible that built America. In concise fashion, how would you contrast and compare the Geneva Bible translation with the Authorized Version, King James Bible? I believe they are doing this fundamentally, to establish and maintain a strict Reformed Covenantal and Post-Millennial Eschatological position. They seem to believe that the AV-King James Bible is misleading and in error with respect to their Theological understanding. What do you think about this?

ANSWER #1117

I agree with you that these publishers are pushing for the amillennial and hyper-Calvinist positions of Reformed theology. Their hardback is $50.00. Ours is $15.00. Someone is using needlessly high prices from the Christians and it's not the Bible For Today's *Defined King James Bible.* You can order Mrs. John Wallnofer's critique of the Geneva Bible called *"Why Not The Geneva Bible?"* You can also order a 50-page article on the Geneva Bible by Brian Finlayson from Canada. It is called *"The Geneva and King James Bibles: Their Historical Context, Features, and Legacies."* Though the Geneva Bible was based on the Textus Receptus in the New Testament, according to the assessment of John Reynolds before King James, it was one of the English translations then in existence in 1604 that was *"not answering to the originals"* of Hebrew, Aramaic, and Greek in a satisfactory manner.

The NIV

QUESTION #1118

I do not know where else to go, so perhaps you can help. The church I attend uses the New International Version (NIV). Bible-based churches are rare here, so my wife and I were blessed to find it. The pastor is a dedicated Southern Baptist, but saved. When I was saved at 41, I tossed my NIV away via the Holy Spirit urgings. I do not want to try to find another church, as this is an awesome chore, so I will try to talk to the pastor. He will not accept a long legal argument so I need the best summary you have that summarizes what is wrong with the NIV. If he does not change Bibles, my wife and I will leave with nowhere to go. Do you have a short summary of what is wrong with the NIV? My wife and I have listened to many of your presentations and I thank you for selling out to God and going all the way with Him.

ANSWER #1118

Not that this one hour summary will convince your pastor of the defects in the NIV and all of the other modern versions, but I think it is a summary of many, many hours of other evidence that I could bring out. It might be something he would listen to in the quietness of his own home. You should listen to it first, and then you would know whether or not to send it to him. It is a "Fourfold King James Bible Defense" in A One Hour Video by Pastor D. A. Waite, Th.D., Ph.D. It is a summary of this important subject. The outline of the presentation is as follows:

1. Bible Preservation
2. King James Bible's Superior Hebrew & Greek Texts
3. King James Bible's Superior Translators

> 4. King James Bible's Superior Translation Technique
> 5. King James Bible's Superior Theology
> Click the LINK below to view the video tape:
> http://vimeo.com/15427264

I'm glad you are able to listen to our messages on the **BROWN BOX** at our website, BibleForToday.org. If you leave this church and can't find a good one that is based on the King James Bible and its underlying Hebrew, Aramaic, and Greek Words, you are invited to attend our services on the **BROWN BOX** at our website, BibleForToday.org on Sundays at 10 a.m. and 1:30 p.m. (Eastern) and Thursdays at 8 p.m. (Eastern).

The N. T. Recovery Version

QUESTION #1119

Sunday, after my presentation on the King James Bible, I was asked about *"The New Testament Recovery Version."* I am not familiar with this version. Do you have any information about this version?

ANSWER #1119

"The New Testament Recovery Version" can be seen on the Internet. It is based on the Gnostic Critical Greek New Testament Text. Because of this, it has over 8,000 differences with the Greek Text underlying the King James Bible. It also has over 356 doctrinal passages that are corrupt. The Internet site: http://online.recoveryversion.org/Outlines.asp?bookid=50 gives the entire New Testament online. For example, in 1 Timothy 3:16, they reject *"GOD* [THEOS] *was manifest in the flesh."* but just *"HE WHO was manifested in the flesh"* in place of *"GOD."* This is a denial of the incarnation of the Lord Jesus Christ. It is also a denial of His Deity. In Philippians 4:13, where the true text reads, *"I can do all things through CHRIST,"* this version reads *"in HIM who"* and leaves out *"CHRIST."* Stay away from that Gnostic perversion of the truth of God!

What About Study Bibles?

QUESTION #1120

Which study Bible, if any, could you recommend? Is there one or more that you would say is more accurate?

ANSWER #1120

I certainly recommend our *Defined King James Bible* which is a "study Bible" in that it defines accurately uncommon words found in the King James Bible. A sound and true study Bible with notes and outlines is difficult to recommend. There are always downsides to any. I have been using the *OLD*

SCOFIELD REFERENCE BIBLE for many years. It has notes that I agree with as to dispensational truth, pre-tribulation rapture, the millennial reign of Christ, and many other things. But if you use this study Bible, you should disregard any footnotes or center marginal notes that suggest a change in the wording of the King James Bible in favor of the false Gnostic Critical Greek Text.

Dr. C. I. Scofield, with all of his sound theology on other matters, wrongly thought that the Westcott and Hort's Gnostic Critical Greek text was right and the Traditional Received Greek text underlying our King James Bible was wrong. So he has notes here and there that he and his editors believe "correct" some of the words of the King James Bible to conform them with his false and favored Gnostic Critical Greek Text. Just disregard these notes. Most of his other notes are very helpful. With that caution, I would recommend the *OLD SCOFIELD REFERENCE BIBLE* (not the *NEW SCOFIELD BIBLE* which changes many of the good notes found in the *OLD SCOFIELD REFERENCE BIBLE*).

CHAPTER VI
QUESTIONS ABOUT
GREEK MANUSCRIPTS

Editions of the Textus Receptus
QUESTION #1121

I read that there have been many editions of the Textus Receptus. The article stated that the King James Version translators used one of the many editions. Is that true? And if so, how do we know that the particular edition that was used by the King James Bible translators is accurate?

ANSWER #1121

Yes, there are a number editions of the Traditional or Textus Receptus Greek New Testament Text. Though not precisely the same, they are very close to each other. However, all of these editions of the Textus Receptus are different in about 1,500 to 1,800 places from the so-called "Majority Greek Text." They are also different in over 8,000 places from the Gnostic Critical Greek Text which is called either the Westcott and Hort Text, the Nestle/Aland Text, or the United Bible Societies Text. These last three Greek texts differ in many thousands of places among themselves.

The main beginning edition of the Traditional Text was that of Erasmus in 1516. Around the same time there was a Complutensian Polyglot. There was also a Stephens edition of 1550. The Textus Receptus used as the basis for the King James Bible was Beza's 5th edition of 1598. This was 82 years after the Erasmus edition of 1516. These extra 82 years allowed various spelling differences and other things to be worked out.

Though Dr. Frederick Scrivener listed 190 places where the King James editors chose another Greek source, Beza's 5th edition of 1598 was what was used in all other places. Since the Greek New Testament text has over 140,000 words, 190 differences are but a very minor difference.

Based upon all of the study I have made on this subject, it is my personal belief that these Greek Words that underlie the King James Bible are the preserved original Words of the Greek New Testament and are therefore authentic. Because of this, I believe the Gnostic Critical Greek editions which change these Words in over 8,000 places are not to be trusted. They are to be totally rejected where they differ with the Words underlying the King James Bible.

Luke 2:14 in the Greek Text

QUESTION #1122

About six months ago, I wrote to you about a criticism my church pastor has about the King James Bible translation of Luke 2:14. I agree with the King James Bible's rendering of this. He seems to think that the King James translation causes people to struggle because of the view it gives of God. How would you answer this?

The English Standard Version (ESV)
Luke 2:14
"Glory to God in the highest, and on earth peace __among those with whom he is pleased__!"

The King James Bible (KJB)
Luke 2:14
"Glory to God in the highest, and on earth peace, __good will toward men__."

ANSWER 1122

Your agreement with the reading of the King James Bible is correct, and your interpretation is certainly one which is in line with the King James Bible's underlying Words. There is one Greek Word in this verse which makes the difference. EUDOKIA *"good will"* is the correct word which has the support of the manuscript evidence. It is in the nominative as the subject of the idea, *"good will toward men."* On the other hand, EUDOKIAS *"of good will"* is the incorrect word used in the modern English Bibles such as the English Standard Version (ESV) and others. It lacks the support of manuscript evidence. It is in the genitive to go with literally *"men of good will."*

The specific and overwhelming manuscript evidence for EUDOKIA is given by Dr. Jack Moorman in page 172 of his book, *Early Manuscripts, Church Fathers, and the Authorized Version* (BFT #3230 @ $20.00 + $8.00 S&H). Dean Burgon has listed this as one of three crucial interpretations in the New Testament. The other two are 2 Timothy 3:16 and Mark 16:9-20. The evidence of this verse was very important to Dean Burgon and it should be very important to us as well.

New Testament Greek Texts

QUESTION #1123

Can you please advise, first, as to which Greek text (by date) provides the best actual representation of the Textus Receptus? I've grown confused trying to decipher the various opinions found on the Internet. Second, can you please advise as to whether there is a digital version of the Textus Receptus with accents available for download?

ANSWER #1123

I believe the best New Testament Greek Text is that of Dr. Frederick Scrivener. We have the smaller printed copies available as **BFT #471 @ $15.00 + $7.00 S&H.** We also have a larger printed edition showing the changes made in the Westcott and Hort Gnostic Critical Greek Text as well as the footnotes and appendix used in Dr. Scrivener's original book. This is **BFT #1670 @ $35.00 + $8.00 S&H.** To get a digital version of this Greek Text, you can go to Logos Bible Program and get Scrivener's TR online with accents. The LINK you can use is: http://www.logos.com/products

Textus Receptus Vs. Majority Text

QUESTION #1124

Can you point me to a definitive resource which clearly describes both the Textus Receptus and the Majority Text? I've read some pages that say they are synonymous, while others say they are not.

ANSWER #1124

In my book, *Defending the King James Bible* (**BFT #1594 @ $12.00 + $8.00 S&H**), I differentiate between the Textus Receptus and the so-called "Majority Text." Before the late 1980's, the Textus Receptus and the "Majority Text" were both called the"Majority Text." After Hodges and Farstad published, in the 1980's, their so-called "Majority Text," they took the name of "Majority Text" as an exclusive name. It is no longer called the Textus Receptus. Their Greek version changed the Textus Receptus Greek Text in 1,500 to 1,800 places. There is also a second so-called "Majority Text" called the Robinson/Pierpoint "Majority" text. There is also a third so-called "Majority Text" which is being prepared as I am writing this by Dr. Wilbur Pickering. It should be pointed out that neither of these three different so-called "Majority Texts" consists of a "majority" (that is, over 2,750 Greek manuscripts that agree with their text) of the over 5,500 preserved manuscripts now in our possession. This is why I refer to all three of these editions as "*so-called Majority Texts.*"

The Date Of The Sinai Manuscript
QUESTION #1125
Codex-Sinaiticus was written in the 4th century A.D., am I right? The Greek Orthodox Church says that codex-Sinaiticus is the oldest manuscript.
ANSWER #1125
It is one of the oldest. Though it is not dated, it is estimated to be composed sometime in the 4th century A.D.

The Sinai Greek Manuscript
QUESTION #1126
Does the Sinai codex contain parts of the Old Testament, or only the New Testament?
ANSWER #1126
http://www.codex-sinaiticus.net/en/codex/content.aspx gives you information on the books of the Old Testament, the New Testament, the Apocrypha, and a few other books that are included in the 4th Century A.D. Sinai Greek Manuscript.

Agreement of Apograph MSS
QUESTION #1127
I'm curious if you have an article that addresses the following. It is stated that no two manuscripts of any Greek manuscript copies (*apographs*) agree perfectly. When discussing and defending the Authorized Version, that comes up frequently. What is your comment on this?
ANSWER #1127
That might be true in the case of both the Textus Receptus manuscripts as well as the Gnostic Critical Text manuscripts. In this regard, the differences and contradictions in the Gnostic Critical Greek Text number into the thousands, whereas the differences in the Textus Receptus Text contain only slight and minor differences. Though there are variations in them, they are not as many and they are not as drastic. If 8 have one reading and 2 depart, it is easy to conclude that the 8 were correct and the 2 were wrong. This is the case in evaluating differences in the Textus Receptus manuscripts.

Dates of the New Testament
QUESTION #1128
Do you know the dates when the oldest copies of New Testament Scriptures were written? I need some dates to deal with the usual objections

such as *"the Bible was changed a few hundred years ago"* or *"the Bible was written hundreds of years after Jesus."*

ANSWER #1128

The New Testament Greek was completed about 90 or 100 A.D. The **Words** of the Traditional Received Greek Text go back to that date regardless of the age of the **material** on which those **Words** were written. Don't be fooled by the date of the **materials.** For example, the Vatican and Sinai manuscripts claim a date of the 4th century A.D. for their **materials**, but their **Words** have been completely altered and doctored in line with various Gnostic heresies. This has been shown by many evidences and proofs which I will not go into in this answer. On the other hand, the **materials**, on which the Textus Receptus Words appear might be much later than the **materials** on which the Gnostic Greek Text were placed, but the **Words** of the Textus Receptus go back to the original **Words** of the originals. Again, I will not go into the evidences and proofs of this. This is a very important distinction to bear in mind.

Greek Manuscripts

QUESTION #1129

As I was thinking and studying, I thought of a question I wanted to ask you. I was thinking of how the Sinaiticus and Vaticanus were found in Alexandria, Egypt, and do not agree with each other. That brought to me the obvious question, in how many different places was the Textus Receptus found, and yet there is general close agreement? There had to be 100's or even 1000's of Greek manuscripts and yet those copies of the Textus Receptus are in general agreement.

ANSWER #1129

If you have Dean Burgon's book, *The Traditional Text* (**BFT #1159 @ $16.00 + $8.00 S&H**), pages 50 and 52, you can see the variety of manuscripts and sources of those manuscripts *"from widely sundered regions."* (p. 52). He mentions places such as (1) Palestine, (2) Constantinople; (3) Alexandria; (4) Pelusium (near the Nile); (5) Nonnus of Panopolis in the Thebaid; (6) Lyons in Gaul; and (7) Antioch. (p. 52). I have numbered these places, but it gives you the idea that the Traditional Text (the Textus Receptus) comes from sources all over the then-known world, rather than just like Vatican and Sinai which were from the Alexandria, Egypt, area only and were corrupted by the followers of Gnosticism. It should be pointed out that Alexandria, Egypt, was also the headquarters for the Gnostic Religion. This explains why the changes found in both the Vatican and Sinai manuscripts are generally in line with the heresies found in the Gnostic religion.

Greek Text Colophons
QUESTION #1130
I wanted to know about colophons. In some English (King James Bible) Bibles the colophons are included at the closing of the Pauline Epistles. I was looking in my Greek text, and I didn't see them included in that text. However I believe that I have heard that they are in the Textus Receptus. Do you have any information on them? I would be curious as to any information that I could get on those.

ANSWER #1130
These colophons sometimes explain the place where the letter was written, the stenographer, or some other comment. From all that I can see, the colophons occur in Stephens 1550 Greek only. I have read two opinions on them. Dr. Floyd Jones thinks they're genuine. He was going to speak on this topic a year or so ago at the DBS, but was unable to come at the last minute. The Trinitarian Bible Society's recent article took the position that they are not valid. I'm sorry, but I haven't studied them enough to come down on one side or another. We all must do some more study on these colophons.

A Byzantine Type Text?
QUESTION #1131
Is it right to say that the Textus Receptus is a "Byzantine" form of the Greek Text?

ANSWER #1131
Yes, *"Byzantine"* is another name rightly used to describe the Received, Textus Receptus, or Traditional Greek Text. Constantinople was the capital of the Byzantium empire. In that city were found many hundreds of Greek manuscripts since this city was the capital of the entire Greek Empire whose language was Greek. For this reason, the city used these Greek manuscripts in their Greek Orthodox Churches. This city, formerly called Byzantium, was the source of many of the Received Traditional Text manuscripts. It was not the **exclusive** source of **only** those manuscripts used by the so-called "majority text." This term has been stolen by some to limit its use to **only** what they call the so-called *"majority text."* I disagree with these *"majority text"* people on this and on many other points. So beware of this difference.

Is the Greek Text From Latin?

QUESTION #1132

I heard Dr. James M. Philips of Discover the Word Ministry, Bakersfield, California, saying that:

> "*The Textus Receptus is not a Greek text, but just a translation of the Latin Vulgate from Jerome.*"

What's your answer to that?

ANSWER #1132

This is an entirely false statement by Philips. It is without a shred of documentation to back it up. The entire New Testament was written entirely in the Greek language, not the Latin language. It is false to say that it was a "*translation of the Latin Vulgate from Jerome.*" Since Jerome's Latin Vulgate was made up in 382 A.D. and following, this would mean that our Greek New Testament would not be in existence until after 382 A.D. rather than the fact that it was completed in 90 to 100 A.D. This is heresy of the worst sort! The reverse of this is true. The Latin Vulgate of Jerome was taken from the Greek manuscripts of the New Testament. There are presently more than 5,500 Greek manuscripts in existence, far more than Latin manuscripts which were translations of the Greek originals.

The Didache & Other Gnostic Books

QUESTION #1133

Is it worth studying the story of the Didache? Some say it was the first Christian handbook of the apostles. Is that true?

ANSWER #1133

Some have said this, but I think we should be very careful in accepting the authenticity of this document. Because of this, I do not think it is "*worth studying.*" I don't believe it was the first Christian handbook of the apostles. Since it is not one of the books of the New Testament, I don't believe it should be exalted in any way lest it seem to contradict the Words of God as given in the New Testament. I believe it was a Gnostic book which cannot be trusted.

New Testament Corruptions

QUESTION #1134

Could you direct me to a "source" that would have a list of passages that are corrupt? Thank you for your much appreciated help.

ANSWER #1134

You can find about **168** of the more important of the **356 doctrinal passages** in Chapter V of my book, *Defending the King James Bible* (BFT #1594 @ $12.00 + $8.00 S&H).   You can find all **356** of the **doctrinal passages** (almost 200 pages) in Dr. Jack Moorman's book, *Early Manuscripts, Church Fathers and the Authorized Version* (BFT #3230 @ $20.00 + $8.00 S&H).   He has all of the manuscript authorities listed as well.   To find the entire list of 8,000 **word differences** between the Textus Receptus Words and those of the corrupt Gnostic Critical text readings, you can find them in Dr. Jack Moorman's book, *8,000 Differences Between the Textus Receptus Text and the Critical Text* (BFT #3084 @ $20.00 + $8.00 S&H).

New Testament Manuscripts

QUESTION #1135

Dr. Waite, what manuscript evidence is there for this Bible version issue? What website can I go to find this information? I have all of Dean Burgon's books, but I am not finding all of what I need. Any help you can provide would be appreciated.

ANSWER #1135

In answer to this further question, as I have stated in a former question, let me repeat it here:

> *"You can find about **168** of the more important of the **356** doctrinal passages in Chapter V of my book, Defending the King James Bible (BFT #1594 @ $12.00 + $8.00 S&H).   You can find all **356** of the doctrinal passages (almost 200 pages) in Dr. Jack Moorman's book, Early Manuscripts, Church Fathers and the Authorized Version (BFT #3230 @ $20.00 + $8.00 S&H).   He has all of the manuscript authorities listed as well.   To find the entire list of 8,000 word differences between the Textus Receptus Words and those of the corrupt Gnostic Critical text readings, you can find them in Dr. Jack Moorman's book, 8,000 Differences Between the Textus Receptus Text and the Critical Text (BFT #3084 @ $20.00 + $8.00 S&H)."*

Did Scrivener Change the Greek?
QUESTION #1136

I know that you are very busy, but if you have the time, I have a few questions. I read that Scrivener, in his edition of the Textus Receptus, **changed the text** in some places to match the Alexandrian text-types. Is this true? Do we have the same text available to us today that was used by Tyndale and the King James translators? I have heard that the Greek text was correct when the King James Bible translators used it, but that it was later partially corrupted, which is what we have today. This is very important for me to know.

ANSWER #1136

1.   I do not believe that Dr. Scrivener changed the Received text to match the false Alexandrian text.

2.   I believe we have the same Greek New Testament text that underlies the King James Bible that underlay the Tyndale Bible.

3.   I do not believe that the Received Greek Text used by the King James Bible has been corrupted today. You can still buy it in smaller print as **BFT #471** @ **$14.00 + $8.00 S&H** or in a larger print with Scrivener's indications where the Critical text changed the Textus Receptus and all of his footnotes as **BFT #1670 @ $35.00 + $8.00 S&H**.

Tischendorf's Sinai Manuscript
QUESTION #1137

What effect did Tischendorf's discovery of the Sinai manuscript (Aleph) have on the compilers of the King James Bible?

ANSWER #1137

Since Tischendorf discovered this manuscript in 1859, the King James Translators knew nothing about that discovery since they published their translation in 1611. They had known of the incorrect Gnostic Critical Greek readings from other manuscripts that were similar to those of the Sinai, but rejected them as not being sound. They were right in their rejection of these.

Erasmus Criticism, Is it Proper?
QUESTION #1138

There are many people who criticize Erasmus in a number of ways. Is it true to say that Erasmus was the compiler of our Textus Receptus Greek text that underlies our King James Bible?

ANSWER #1138

In the first place, it is false to say that the King James Bible's New Testament Greek Text was that of Erasmus of 1516. It was rather Beza's 5th edition Greek Text of 1598. This was 82 years after that of Erasmus. In the second place, Erasmus' so-called "humanism" and a strong "Roman Catholic" position has been overrated. Erasmus was not an atheistic "humanist" as we think of humanists today. He was a humanitarian who helped many people. Erasmus was not a strong Roman Catholic as seen from these facts: (1) his books were banned by the Pope; (2) he refused a Cardinal's hat; (3) he was not buried in a Roman Catholic cemetery, but in a Protestant cemetery; (4) instead of keeping his New Testament in Latin only (which was the only language that Rome preferred in his days), he printed a parallel New Testament with Latin on one side and Greek on the other.

Why Use Beza's 1598 Greek Edition?

QUESTION #1139

As a Textus Receptus (TR) Bible translator, I am often asked why I use Textus Receptus as my underlining text. Even though I can easily answer that question, I have trouble answering some other related questions. Not knowing anyone else who is informed on the subject as good as you are, I decided to ask those questions to you. To make things simple, I will ask one question at a time. Please be assured these are genuine and sincere questions. I am not trying to catch you in a word. Your help would be greatly appreciated.

The Dean Burgon Society's Articles of Faith state the following:

"We believe that the Texts which are the closest to the original autographs of the Bible are the Traditional Masoretic Hebrew Text for the Old Testament, and the traditional Greek Text for the New Testament underlying the King James Version (as found in "The Greek Text Underlying The English Authorized Version of 1611."

Why do you believe *The Greek Text Underlying The English Authorized Version of 1611* is closest to original autographs? Why not Stephen's 1550 or Beza's 1598, or Elzevir's 1624 or some other?

ANSWER #1139

According to Dr. Scrivener (who examined this Greek text carefully), the King James Bible used (with only 190 exceptions that he cites in his appendix) Beza's 5th edition, 1598. We believe by 1598, all of the copying mistakes had been corrected since Erasmus' 1516 edition and Stephens' 1550 edition. Elzevir's 1624 edition had not come out as yet by 1611. In the main, I do not believe there are very many variations among these Traditional Texts.

1 John 5:7-8 Verses Are Genuine
QUESTION #1140
I have a question for you about some information floating about on the Internet concerning the manuscript evidence for 1 John 5:7-8. Has anyone ever written a statement or article about these verses? I don't know if anyone has written a clarification on this, but it would help out if someone did. It would give us a bit more credence.

ANSWER #1140
Though an entire book has been written on the evidence supporting 1 John 5:7-8 by Michael Maynard (which book is out of print, but is being brought back into print by the author), I believe the clearest and most succinct summary of the evidence on 1 John 5:7-8 has been written by Dr. Jack Moorman, one of our church's missionaries and a resident now of the UK. It is **BFT #2249 @ $4.00 + $2.00 S&H**. The title is *1 John 5:7-8 Authenticated & Summarized* by Dr. Jack Moorman.

CHAPTER VII
QUESTIONS ABOUT
BEHAVIOR OF CHRISTIANS

Is It Wrong to Mock the Dead?
QUESTION #1141

Is it wrong to mock the dead? Say that someone is analyzing something that someone has written and makes fun of, mocks, and belittles that person. If that person is dead, are there any consequences about that? Is there anything in the Bible about that?

ANSWER #1141

I don't think we should mock the persons as such, but certainly I think we can disagree and refute what they might have written down, or spoken, including their evil works. We can refute Charles Darwin's writings, his racism, and so forth. 1 Thessalonians 5:21 tells us to *"Prove* [test out and scrutinize and examine] *all things; hold fast that which is good."* The Bible also tells us to: *"have no fellowship with the unfruitful works of darkness, but rather reprove* [bring to light and expose] *them."* (See Ephesians 5:11.)

Should I Fight People on the Street?
QUESTION #1142

If I were to box someone, people in the street would be watching me and wonder what kind of a Christian I am. However, I feel kind of stupid. I didn't fight him. I am 36 years old. The person is 42 or 43. I don't want to give a bad impression to the people because I am afraid it will affect my preaching and teaching ministry to them. What do you think of that?

ANSWER #1142

Your reasoning is good. I'm glad you'll go to the police tomorrow about this man who is attacking you.

Is it Wise to Burn the Koran?

QUESTION #1143

What do you think of this pastor who publicly burned a copy of the Koran recently?

ANSWER #1143

Though he has the freedom to do as he sees fit, it seems to me that this is a very unwise thing to do either publicly or privately.

Is Christian Activism Wrong?

QUESTION #1144

What do you think about Christian activism? Do you think it is wrong for Christians to meet and protest (at prayer meetings, by preaching, or even marching with signs) wicked and sinful activities such as abortion, false churches, naked body scanners, and GMO foods? What about unconstitutional things like: police check points, abusive police, illegal wiretapping, etc.? There is a group here in Charleston that is going to start demonstrating such things.

ANSWER #1144

If a Christian is led to take such actions, as long as no Biblical standards are violated, that is a personal decision for him to make. I used to protest such various things when I was connected with Dr. Carl McIntire, but have not done so recently. I do not think it usually does much good. To each his own, however.

What Is the N.T. Policy of Giving?

QUESTION #1145

Are you for the New Testament in freewill giving, or for the Old Testament principle of levitical tithing? I am not being critical, but need to know. Thank you.

ANSWER #1145

I am not opposed to New Testament tithing as a good beginning though nowhere is it commanded in the New Testament, but I am most especially for the New Testament freewill giving which is giving "*as God hath prospered*" us (1 Corinthians 16:2). Every born-again Christian should give at least **something** "*as God hath prospered.*"

How Should the Bible Be Studied?

QUESTION #1146

I came across your yearly Bible reading plan. What would you recommended for a new believer such as me, who has only been saved for about thirty-two weeks or so now? Should I just focus primarily on reading the 66 books of the Holy Bible, or should I try to dive deeper into it with studies? I know with our world, time is short, so it would be wise for me to make the best decision. The real problem I have with study is, I don't understand a lot of the Words in the Bible. For example:

The Book of Matthew

Chapter I.

1. Generation | 2. Son | 3. Begat | 4. Husband | 5. Born | 6. Birth | 7. Christ | 8. Child | 9. Holy | 10. Ghost | 11. Just | 12. Willing | 13. Publick | 14. Example | 15. Minded | 16. Privily 17. Thought | 18. angel | 19. appeared | 20. Dream | 21. Conceived | 22. Save | 23. People | 24. Sins | 25. Fulfilled | 26. Spoken | 27. Prophet | 28. Virgin | 29. Interpreted | 30. Bidden | 31. Wife |

The Epistle of Jude

1. Servant | 2. Sanctified | 3. Preserved | 4. Mercy | 5. Peace | 6. Love | 7. Multiplied | 8. Beloved | 9. Diligence | 10. Salvation | 11. Common | 12. Needful | 13. Exhort | 14. Earnestly | 15. Contend | 16. Faith | 17. Delivered | 18. Saints | 19. Crept | 20. Unawares | 21. Ordained | 22. Condemnation | 23. Ungodly | 24. Grace | 25. Lasciviousness | 26. Denying | 27. Lord | 28. Remembrance | 29. Knew | 30. Saved | 31. People | 32. Destroyed | 33. Believed | 34. Kept | 35. First | 36. Estate | 37. Habitation | 38. Reserved | 39. Everlasting | 40. Chains | 41. Darkness | 42. Judgment | 43. Great | 44. Fornication | 45. Strange | 46. Flesh | 47. Example | 48. Suffering | 49. Vengeance | 50. Eternal | 51. Filthy | 52. Defile | 53. Despise | 54. Dominion | 55. Speak | 56. Evil | 57. Dignities | 58. Archangel | 59. Contending | 60. Devil | 61. Disputed | 62. Railing | 63. Accusation | 64. Rebuke | 65. Naturally | 66. Brute | 67. Corrupt | 68. Greedily | 69. Error | 70. Reward | 71. Perished | 72. Gainsaying | 73. Charity | 74. Fear | 75. Shame | 76. Wandering | 77. Saints | 78. Execute | 79. Convince | 80. Deeds 81. Committed | 82. Hard | 83. Speeches | 84. Sinners | 85. Murmurers | 86. Complainers | 87. Lusts | 88. Swelling | 89. Admiration | 90. Advantage | 91. Apostles | 92. Mockers | 93. Time | 94. Separate | 95. Sensual | 96. Building | 97. Holy | 98. Praying | 99. Life | 100. Compassion | 101. Difference | 102. Hating | 103. Faultless | 104. Presence | 105. Glory | 106. Exceeding | 107. Joy | 108. Wise | 109. God | 110. Saviour | 111. Majesty | 112. Power | Those are just a list of words I don't understand in those chapters or books.

ANSWER #1146

I am glad you are genuinely born-again, saved, and redeemed by faith in the Lord Jesus Christ. *The Defined King James Bible* you ordered should help you in understanding many uncommon words. I hope it will arrive in a few days or so. I think you should have a regular daily Bible **reading** of at least 85 verses each day to read the entire Bible through in one year.

After the Bible **reading** you can spend some extra time, if you wish, in Bible **study**. Here are my recommendations:

1. Use my Yearly Bible Reading schedule to read the Bible through once a year at 85 verses per day.

2. In addition, begin by studying the Gospel of John each day until you are finished with it.

3. Then study the book of Romans, and other New Testament books.

4. On your Internet, go to our BibleForToday.org website, and click on the **BROWN BOX** and listen as I preach verse by verse from Romans through Revelation.

5. Use the definitions of various uncommon words in the *Defined King James Bible* so some of these words you have listed will become clear. For other words, you can use a good English dictionary like *Webster's*.

6. Don't think you can learn everything all at once. It takes time. You can feel free to phone me at **856-854-4747** if I can help you at any time.

How Much Do We Love Lord Jesus?

QUESTION #1147

How much do you love Jesus?

ANSWER #1147

I love the Lord Jesus Christ with all of my heart and seek to serve Him with all my spirit, my soul, and my body. Some of the following verses define for us a measuring stick for our "love" for the Lord Jesus Christ:

John 14:15

*"If ye **love me**, **keep** my commandments."*

John 14:21

*"He that hath my commandments, and **keepeth them, he it is that loveth me**: and he that loveth me shall be loved of my Father, and I will love him, and will manifest myself to him."*

> **John 14:23**
>
> *"Jesus answered and said unto him, **If a man love me, he will keep my words**: and my Father will love him, and we will come unto him, and make our abode with him."*
>
> **John 14:24**
>
> *"He that **loveth me not keepeth not** my sayings: and the word which ye hear is not mine, but the Father's which sent me."*
>
> **1 John 4:19**
>
> "We love him, because he first loved us."

Should We Donate Our Organs?
QUESTION #1148

I don't think it is wise to donate your organs after you die. What do you think about this?

ANSWER #1148

Thank you for this information you have written about organ donations. I agree with you that we should be very careful about this, not only because of the costs that may be involved, but also about other matters.

Here are some of my thoughts about organ donation. If you wanted to donate your heart, for example, the heart would have to be alive and working for it to work in another patient. If it would have to be alive, the doctors would have to kill you first in order to remove your working heart. But what if you were not yet ready to die? What if you had some more years yet to live? You would have no choice in the matter. The doctor who guessed that you could only live for a few more hours or days, would be able to *"harvest"* your heart while it was still working and you were still living. This *"harvesting"* would kill you, yet the doctor would not be charged with murder. This entire operation seems very strange to me. Remember, the body (including all of its organs) for the born-again Christian is the temple of God the Holy Spirit. Because of this, born-again Christians should be very careful how they use their bodies, both in their lives, and at their deaths.

What Are Pastoral Standards?
QUESTION #1149

I know of a preacher who is seeking a church. How can you help find him a church?

> **ANSWER #1149**
> I don't know of a church to recommend for this pastor at this time. Before I would recommend any man to a church, I would have to know his position on the King James Bible and its underlying Hebrew, Aramaic, and Greek Words. I would also want to see his extensive doctrinal statement so I know what his various positions are on Biblical separation and many other things. Our own Bible For Today Baptist Church's Articles of Faith are found on the following link: http://www.biblefortoday.org/bft_articles_faith.htm if anyone would want to look at them to see what I believe. I could not recommend anyone to a local church who did not hold my own doctrinal position.

Answering Critics
QUESTION #1150
How often do you get responded with hostility when you try to show the truth even to your closest brethren whether it's about the King James Bible, false teachers, or other things?

ANSWER #1150
Hostility comes often to those of us who stick closely to Biblical truth among those who do not wish to stick so closely. Don't let it get you down. Be glad the Lord has given you insight into His Words. Here's the advice that the Lord Jesus Christ gave to His disciples about the Pharisees who were "*offended.*" Matthew 15:12-14:

> "*Then came his disciples, and said unto him, Knowest thou that the Pharisees were offended, after they heard this saying? But he answered and said, Every plant, which my heavenly Father hath not planted, shall be rooted up. **Let them alone**: they be blind leaders of the blind. And if the blind lead the blind, both shall fall into the ditch.*"

To those who are "*offended*" in our Biblical positions, we should follow the Lord Jesus Christ's counsel and "*let them alone.*"

How to Deal With Homosexuals
QUESTION #1151
I was wanting to know if you could give me verses from the Bible about what the Bible has to say about a man who is more like a woman in how he talks, how he walks, and how he dresses. A friend of mine has a nephew who acts like a girl. I've told her he is gay. When they are all together for a family

dinner, they would all pray at the end of the night holding hands. I don't take part in that and have told my friend that I can't. I am looking for verses I can show my friend where it is wrong to fellowship with people like this. It is a problem between my friend and me.

ANSWER #1151

If this man is indeed a homosexual and not a born-again Christian, the Biblical principle of separation should immediately go into practice. It is clearly taught in 2 Corinthians 6:14-17. Here are the verses about separating from unbelievers and *"unrighteous"* people (like homosexuals):

2 Corinthians 6:14-17

"Be ye not unequally yoked together with unbelievers: for what fellowship hath righteousness with __unrighteousness__? and what communion hath light with darkness? And what concord hath Christ with Belial? or what part hath he that believeth with an infidel? And what agreement hath the temple of God with idols? for ye are the temple of the living God; as God hath said, I will dwell in them, and walk in them; and I will be their God, and they shall be my people. __Wherefore come out from among them, and be ye separate__, saith the Lord, and touch not the unclean thing; and I will receive you."

Here are some verses that call for separation from those who are supposed born-again Christians who commit **PORNEIA**. This is usually translated *"fornication"* or *"fornicator"* but also in a wider sense includes homosexuals and other deviate sexual acts.

1 Corinthians 5:9-11

"I wrote unto you in an epistle __not to company with fornicators__: Yet not altogether with the fornicators of this world, or with the covetous, or extortioners, or with idolaters; for then must ye needs go out of the world. But now I have written unto you __not to keep company, if any man that is called a brother be a fornicator__, or covetous, or an idolater, or a railer, or a drunkard, or an extortioner; __with such an one no not to eat__."

CHAPTER VIII
QUESTIONS ABOUT THE
CHINESE UNION VERSION

Meaning of "Souls" in CUV
QUESTION #1152
We have a question about the translation of *"eight souls"* in 1 Peter 3:20.

1 Peter 3:20

*"Which sometime were disobedient, when once the longsuffering of God waited in the days of Noah, while the ark was a preparing, wherein few, that is, **eight souls** were saved by water."*

The Chinese Union Version (CUV) translated these words, *"eight people."* Can we translate *"eight souls"* literally?

ANSWER #1152
The Greek word for *"souls"* is PSYCHAI (which is the plural of PSYCHE). That Greek word means literally *"souls."* They are using dynamic equivalence to make it *"people."* It is literally the word for *"souls."* You are correct to translate it as *"souls,"* regardless of what the CUV has done.

Three Questions on the CUV
QUESTION #1153
We have three questions. Please help us:

1) Romans 12:17 *"Recompense to no man evil for evil. Provide things **honest** in the sight of all men."*

CUV translates *"**honest**"* as *"beautiful things."* I found that the Greek does have *"beautiful,"* but I don't know if there's *"beautiful"* in old English (14th century)?

2) 1 Corinthians 2:10 *"But God hath revealed them unto us by his Spirit: for the Spirit **searcheth** all things, yea, the deep things of God."*

CUV translated *"searcheth"* to *"penetrate."*

3) 1 Corinthians 4:8 Now ye are full, now ye are rich, ye have reigned as kings without us: and I would **to God** ye did reign, that we also might reign with you.

CUV didn't translated *"to God"* I cannot find in Greek.

ANSWER #1153

Here are brief answers to your three questions:

1. **Romans 12:17** There are many meanings of KALOS, but *"**honest, purity of heart and life, morally good**"* are also possible.

Here are the various meanings of "honest" (KALOS) in this verse, The King James Bible translated it **"honest" 5 times**:

2570 kalos {kal-os'}

of uncertain affinity; TDNT - 3:536,402; adj

AV - good 83, better 7, **honest 5**, meet 2, goodly 2, misc 3; 102

1) beautiful, handsome, excellent, eminent, choice, surpassing,
   precious, useful, suitable, commendable, admirable
   1a) beautiful to look at, shapely, magnificent
   1b) good, excellent in its nature and characteristics, and
      therefore well adapted to its ends
      1b1) genuine, approved
      1b2) precious
      1b3) joined to names of men designated by their office,
         competent, able, such as one ought to be
      1b4) praiseworthy, noble
   1c) beautiful by reason of purity of heart and life, and hence
      praiseworthy
      1c1) morally good, noble
   1d) honourable, conferring honour
   1e) affecting the mind agreeably, comforting and confirming

---

2. **1 Corinthians 2:10**

Some of the meanings of *"**searcheth**"* (EREUNAO) are as follows:

2045 ereunao {er-yoo-nah'-o}

apparently from 2046 (through the idea of enquiry);

  TDNT - 2:655,255; v

AV - search 6; 6

1) **to search**, examine into

It is *"search"* **6 times in the King James Bible**
"Penetrate" is not meant here.

3. 1 Corinthians 4:8,
Here are some of the meanings of OPHELON translated as *"would to God"*
3785 ophelon {of-el-on}
first person singular of a past tense of 3784; particle
AV - I would 2, I would to God 1, would to God 1; 4
1) would that, where one wishes that a thing had happened which
 has not happened or a thing be done which probably will not be done

Though THEOS (*"God"*) is not in the Greek, the people in 1611 used this expression *"I would to God"* in the sense of I really wish something would happen. They understood very clearly what was meant here with those words.

Increased in Number

QUESTION #1154

We have a question about Acts 16:5: *"And so were the churches established in the faith, and **increased in number** daily."*

CUV translated *"increased in number"* to *"**number of people increased**."* Did *"**number**"* in this verse refer to church or people?

ANSWER #1154

The word for *"**increased**"* is:
4052 **perisseuo** {per-is-syoo'-o}
from 4053; TDNT - 6:58,828; v
AV - abound 17, abundance 3, remain 3, exceed 2, **increase 2**, be left 1, redound 1, misc 10; 39
1) **to exceed a fixed number of measure**, to be left over and above a certain number or measure
 1a) to be over, to remain
 1b) to exist or be at hand in abundance
  1b1) to be great (abundant)
  1b2) a thing which comes in abundance, or overflows unto one,
   something falls to the lot of one in large measure
  1b3) to redound unto, turn out abundantly for, a thing
 1c) to abound, overflow
  1c1) to be abundantly furnished with, to have in abundance,
   abound in (a thing), to be in affluence
  1c2) to be pre-eminent, to excel
  1c3) to excel more than, exceed
 2) to make to abound

2a) to furnish one richly so that he has abundance
2b) to make abundant or excellent
"Abounding" is used of a flower going from a bud to full bloom.
    The word for "**number**" is:
706 arithmos {ar-ith-mos'}
from 142; TDNT - 1:461,78; n m
AV - number 18; 18
1) a fixed and definite number
2) an indefinite number, a multitude
ARITHMOS in turn, is from
142 airo {ah'-ee-ro}
a primary root; TDNT - 1:185,28; v
AV - take up 32, take away 25, take 25, away with 5, lift up 4,
    bear 3, misc 8; 102
1) to raise up, elevate, lift up
    1a) to raise from the ground, take up: stones
    1b) to raise upwards, elevate, lift up: the hand
    1c) to draw up: a fish
2) to take upon one's self and carry what has been raised up, to bear
3) to bear away what has been raised, carry off
    3a) to move from its place
    3b) to take off or away what is attached to anything
    3c) to remove
    3d) to carry off, carry away with one
    3e) to appropriate what is taken
    3f) to take away from another what is his or what is committed
        to him, to take by force
    3g) to take and apply to any use
    3h) to take from among the living, either by a natural death,
        or by violence
    3i) cause to cease

> It does not mention "*number of people increased*," but only "*increased in number*." This could mean the number of churches increased daily (which is what it seems to say). I don't think we should go beyond what the Greek words say by way of **interpretation** and **adding words that are not there**.

A Minister
QUESTION #1155
    Thanks for your message on this Sunday morning. When you preached on Romans 5:25 "*But now I go unto Jerusalem to minister unto the saints.*" You

explained the word "*minister*" (G1247) is "*serve.*" The Chinese Union Version (CUV) translated it as "***offer the supply***." I think we may have to use "*serve*" instead, right?

ANSWER #1155

In Romans 15:25, "***to minister***" is:

1247 **diakoneo** {dee-ak-on-eh'-o}

from 1249; TDNT - 2:81,152; v

AV - minister unto 15, serve 10, minister 7, misc 5; 37

1)) **to be a servant**, attendant, domestic, **to serve**, wait upon

  1a) to minister to one, render ministering offices to

    1a1) to be served, ministered unto

  1b) to wait at a table and offer food and drink to the guests,

    1b1) of women preparing food

  1c) to minister i.e. supply food and necessities of life

    1c1) to relieve one's necessities (e.g. by collecting alms), to provide, take care of, distribute, the things necessary to sustain life

    1c2) to take care of the poor and the sick, who administer the office of a deacon

    1c3) in Christian churches to serve as deacons

  1d) to minister

    1d1) to attend to anything, that may serve another's interests

    1d2) to minister a thing to one, to serve one or by supplying any thing

> I don't think "**offer the supply**" is correct in any way. It should be translated, either "***serve the saints***" or "***minister to the saints***."

"Early and Latter Rain"

QUESTION #1156

James 5:7

"*Be patient therefore, brethren, unto the coming of the Lord. Behold, the husbandman waiteth for the precious fruit of the earth, and hath long patience for it, until he receive **the early and latter rain**.*"

The Chinese Union Version (CUV) translated "***the early and latter rain***" as "***the Autumnal rain and Spring rain***." They also use these words in Deuteronomy 11:14; Job 29:23; Proverbs 16:15; Jeremiah 3:3; Joel 2:23; and Zechariah 10:1. Does the original Greek contain the meaning of "***autumnal***" and "***spring***" in these verses?

1 Peter 1:17

"And if ye call on the Father, who without respect of persons judgeth according to every man's __work__, pass the time of your sojourning here in fear:"

Should we translate it *"__work__"* or *"__deed__"*?

ANSWER #1156

Here are a few comments on these two verses.

1. **James 5:7**: The literal words are *"early"* and *"latter."* The interpretation and dynamic equivalence of those words might be *"autumnal"* and *"spring."* But this is interpretation, not translation.

2. **1 Peter 1:17**: The Greek word is ERGON. *"Work"* is the usual meaning of ERGON. The singular *"work"* (which implies both *"work"* and *"works"*) makes sense. The singular *"deed"* does not make sense. To make sense, it would have to be plural, or *"deeds."* But this word is singular, not plural.

"Love of the Father"
QUESTION #1157
1 John 2:15

"Love not the world, neither the things that are in the world. If any man love the world, __the love of the Father__ is not in him."

The Chinese Union Version (CUV) translation is *"__the heart of loving God, is not in him__"* instead of *"__the love of the Father__"* as in the King James Bible. We think that CUV is wrong, what do you think?

ANSWER #1157

You are correct. The CUV is wrong here. The King James Bible is correct. There is no such wording as *"__the heart of loving God__."* The literal rendering of the Greek words, AGAPE TOU PATROS is *"__the love of the Father__"* which is what the King James Bible has.

Christ "Laid Down" His Life For Us
QUESTION #1158

1 John 3:16 says: *"By this we know love, because he __laid down__ his life for us. And we ought to lay down our lives for the brethren."*

Romans 16:4 says: *"Who have for my life __laid down__ their own necks: unto whom not only I give thanks, but also all the churches of the Gentiles."*

The Chinese Union Version (CUV) translated it *"__gave up__"* in the above

verses instead of "laid down." We prefer to stay with "*laid down.*" Please
advise us about this.

ANSWER #1158
In both 1 John 3:16 and Romans 16:4, the Greek word for "*laid down*" comes from the Greek Word, TITHEMI. In Romans 16:4, it is a compound of TITHEMI (HUPOTITHEMI.) Both words mean "*to deposit or to lay down*" something. There is not the remotest possibility that these Greek words can be "*give up.*" This could only be a figurative meaning. The literal meaning is "*lay down.*"

"Angel" or "Messenger"?
QUESTION #1159
Revelation 1:1 reads: "*Unto the **angel** of the church of Ephesus write; These things saith he that holdeth the seven stars in his right hand who walketh in the midst of the seven golden candlesticks;*" This word, "*angel,*" is also found in Revelation 2:8, 12, 18; 3:1, 7, and 14.

The Chinese Union Version (CUV) translated this word as "*messenger.*" We cannot decided whether to translate it as "*angel*" or "*messenger.*" Please advise.

ANSWER #1159
While it is true that ANGELOS means "*messenger, angel, or envoy,*" as a translation of the word, it seems more appropriate not to interpret it or translate it, but to transliterate it (letter for letter), as our King James Bible has done. This has been done in many proper names such as ADAM, rather than translating it as "dust, or red." And this is so with many other proper names in the Old Testament and New Testament. In Revelation 2 and 3, I believe these "angels" or "messengers" refer to the pastors of these seven churches.

"Against" or "Reprove"?
QUESTION #1160
Revelation 2:4 reads: "*Nevertheless I have somewhat **against** thee, because thou hast left thy first love.*"

The Chinese Union Version (CUV) translates "*against*" as "*reprove.*" Do you think it can be translated to "*reprove,*" "*accuse,*" or "*oppose*"? Please advise.

ANSWER #1160
"*Against*" is the proper translation of this preposition, KATA. It is not a good translation to change this preposition into a verb, "*reprove, accuse, or*

oppose." This is an error. KATA with the genitive (as here) which is indicates "*opposition, antagonism, and in conflict with.*" There is nothing in KATA that rises to the point of the verb, "*reproving.*" That is pure interpretation and adding another Greek verb which does not appear. This preposition KATA with the genitive means "*against*" and that is an excellent translation of it.

CHAPTER IX
QUESTIONS ABOUT THE
NEW TESTAMENT

A Greek Translation Question
QUESTION #1161
In John 1:1, I don't understand, "*and the word was **with God**,*" why "**with God**"? The case is the accusative case, not the instrumental case.
ANSWER #1161
Many times, the Greek preposition, PROS, in the accusative case has the sense of being "*right there, close to, near to, and present with*" God the Father.

The Language of the N.T.
QUESTION #1162
I know the Ancient Romans spoke Latin, so where does the Greek come into play? Did Jesus speak Greek, or Latin? Or did he speak Aramaic? Since the empire was Latin, why wouldn't the New Testament have been written in Latin?
ANSWER #1162
In Jesus' day, both Latin and Greek were current languages. Jesus could have spoken either in Greek or Latin because, as the Son of God, He knows all languages. He spoke in Aramaic (similar to Hebrew), but the writers wrote in Greek, not Latin.

How Can We Learn N.T. Greek?
QUESTION #1163
I was just checking out the "*Beginners Grammar of the Greek New Testament,*" by William Hershey Davis and taught by Pastor D. A. Waite, as hosted on the Dean Burgon Society website at: http://www.deanburgonsociety.org/. The links to the classes are not working for me. How can I find this course?

ANSWER #1163
It is on http://www.biblefortoday.org/greek.htm on the Internet browser. It works fine with my computer. When the LINK comes up, You must click on the words "*class 1*" and so on. To see the Davis textbook, click on the word **TEXT** on the top of the page. It will take you through the entire first year New Testament Greek Course.

Meaning of Greek Words
QUESTION #1164
I hear that the apostle Paul, as concerning the resurrection of Jesus, he used the words "ANASTASIS" and at other times "EGERSIS" (Matthew 27:53, uses EGERSIS too). Which word is right for "resurrection"? ANASTASIS or EGERSIS? And why are two different words used for "resurrection"?

ANSWER #1164
Here are the meanings of both ANASTASIS and EGEIRO from a Greek dictionary from Logos Bible Program. I prefer the word, ANASTASIS, as the clearest word for the bodily resurrection of the Lord Jesus Christ.

ANASTASIS means literally to rise up or to stand up.
386 anastasis {an-as'-tas-is}
from 450; TDNT - 1:371,60; n f
AV - resurrection 39, rising again 1, that should rise 1,
   raised to life again + 1537 1; 42
1) a raising up, rising (e.g. from a seat)
2) a rising from the dead
  2a) that of Christ
  2b) that of all men at the end of this present age
  2c) the resurrection of certain ones in history who were restored
    to life (Heb. 11:35)
  EGEIRO means
1453 egeiro {eg-i'-ro}
  probably akin to the base of 58 (through the idea of collecting
  one's faculties); TDNT - 2:333,195; v
AV - rise 36, raise 28, arise 27, raise up 23, rise up 8,
  rise again 5, raise again 4, misc 10; 141
1) to arouse, cause to rise
  1a) to arouse from sleep, to awake
  1b) to arouse from the sleep of death, to recall the dead to life
  1c) to cause to rise from a seat or bed etc.
  1d) to raise up, produce, cause to appear
    1d1) to cause to appear, bring before the public

1d2) to raise up, stir up, against one
1d3) to raise up i.e. cause to be born
1d4) of buildings, to raise up, construct, erect

1 John 5:7-8 Manuscript Evidence

QUESTION #1165

In the King James Bible, 1 John 5:7-8 reads:

> *"For there are three that bear record [in heaven, the*
> *Father, the Word, and the Holy Ghost: and these three*
> *are one. And there are three that bear witness in earth],*
> the Spirit, and the water, and the blood: and these three
> agree in one."*

But all (or most) of the modern versions, the words in **BOLD** and **UNDERLINED** are missing.

According to Benjamin Wilson in *Emphatic Diaglott*, he wrote:

> *"This text concerning the heavenly witness is not*
> *contained in any Greek manuscript which was written*
> *earlier than the fifteenth century. It is not cited by any of*
> *the ecclesiastical writers; not by any of the early Latin*
> *fathers even when the subjects upon which they treated*
> *would naturally have lead them to appeal to it's*
> *authority. It is therefore evidently spurious."*

Is any of this true?

ANSWER #1165

The best complete answer to this is found in *1 John 5:7-8 Defended as Genuine* (**BFT #2249, 15 pages @ $3.00 + $2.00 S&H**) by Dr. Jack Moorman. Dr. Moorman shows the nine Greek manuscripts that contain it. Contrary to what Wilson says in the question, Dr. Moorman cites a number of Greek and Latin Church Fathers who bear witness to these verses in their entirety.

N. T. Quotes From the O.T.

QUESTION #1166

What percentage of the New Testament is direct quotation of the Old Testament or taken from the Old Testament?

ANSWER #1166

I don't know the percentage, but this LINK gives the New Testament quotes from the Old Testament if you would like to see them.
http://www.kalvesmaki.com/LXX/NTCHART.HTM

Though I do not agree any of these quotes were from the Septuagint, another LINK is here if you would like to see it.
http://www.bible-researcher.com/quote01.html

Greek Word Searches
QUESTION #1167

I was wondering if you could help me with some questions I have about the underlying Greek of the King James Bible. I have a Calvinist friend. I am trying to reach him with the truth. One of the things that he has challenged me on is 2 Peter 3:9:

> "*The Lord is not slack concerning his promise, as some men count slackness; but is longsuffering to us-ward, not willing that any should perish, but that all should come to repentance.*"

My question is: What do I need to be able to see the tense and gender in the original Greek in the New Testament?

ANSWER #1167

The Logos Bible Program would be one thing that would show you. If you had that program, you would find the following: *"Not slack"* is present tense. *"Count slackness"* is present. "Is *longsuffering*" is present. "*Is not willing*" is present. "*That any should perish*" is 2nd aorist. "*Should come*" is aorist.

The Original N.T. Language
QUESTION #1168

I was wondering if any or all of the New Testament could have originally been written in Hebrew. I read that the prologue to Matthew in one of the editions of the Bishops Bible said that Matthew originally wrote the gospel in Hebrew, and that it was still kept in the library of Caesarea.

ANSWER #1168

Many have tried to prove that the New Testament was written in Hebrew first and then made into Greek. I do not believe there is sufficient foundation for this. If indeed the New Testament were to have been written in Hebrew, where are the thousands and thousands of copies of this so-called Hebrew New Testament? They are missing. Yet, as of this writing, there are over 5,500

Greek copies and parts of copies in existence. There are many Hebrew words used here and there in the New Testament. The words written over the cross were in Latin, Hebrew, and Greek. There are only a few words in Aramaic or in Hebrew in the New Testament.

The Epistle From Laodicea
QUESTION #1169

Colossians 4:16 reads:

> *"And when this epistle is read among you, cause that it be read also in the church of the Laodiceans; and that ye likewise read **the epistle from Laodicea**."*

What's *"the epistle from Laodicea"*? Is this epistle in our Bible today?

ANSWER #1169

Though some feel this would be similar to the books of Colossians or Ephesians, there is no such book in our New Testament at present. The LINK below has a full discussion of this question.

http://en.wikipedia.org/wiki/Epistle_to_the_Laodiceans

Give "Strength" or "Strengtheneth"
QUESTION #1170

All the modern versions I check say something like *"I can do all things through Christ who gives me strength."* The King James Bible says *"Which strengtheneth me."* In the original Greek Textus Receptus how would this read? Please shed some light on this for me.

ANSWER #1170

The translation you used makes *"**strength**"* a noun. This is an inaccurate translation. In the Greek, this word is not a noun, but a verb, *"**strengtheneth**."* The Textus Receptus would be translated just as the King James Bible renders it: *"I can do all things through Christ which **strengtheneth** me."* It is the Lord Jesus Christ Who *"strengthened"* Paul and Who alone can *"strengthen"* the genuine Christian today. In 1611, the relative pronoun, *"which,"* was used for people as well as for things. Our English today restricts *"who"* for people and *"which"* for things. Just so long as we recognize that *"which"* was correct in the 1611's language, we have no problem with our King James Bible. It is accurate as a translation.

Terms Used in the Bible
QUESTION #1171
1. Where did the word, *"Bible,"* come from?
2. What language did Jesus speak?
3. B.C. and A.D. are confusing to me. If B.C. means "Before Christ" and A.D. means "After Death," what about after Jesus' birth and what He did in the following years before He died? It couldn't have changed to A.D., if A.D. stands for After Death. Jesus didn't die right after He was born.
ANSWER 1171
1. The word, *"Bible,"* comes from the Greek word, BIBLION which means *"book."*
2. Jesus spoke both Aramaic/Hebrew and Greek.
3. It is not true that A.D. stands for "after death." It stands for two Latin words, ANNO DOMINI, which means *"in the year of our Lord."*

The Meaning of "Denying" Christ
QUESTION #1172
I appreciated learning God's truth last Sunday and wanted to ask a few questions regarding the afternoon study on 2 Timothy 2:12: *"If we deny him, he also will deny us."* I always thought this meant that Jesus would reject us and send us to Hell. Or is this not in the right context since it refers to a "faithful saying": *"If we believe not, yet he abideth faithful, he cannot deny himself."*

What do you think the Word of God means in Matthew 8:22-23? Is this a true picture of the judgment of Hell? However, these people did many things in the name of Christ. Are these the apostate preachers and followers? So they didn't have the Holy Spirit? The Holy Spirit seals us until the day of redemption. Does the backslider still have his place in Heaven? Even if he works true iniquity (knowing that he is doing evil)?

ANSWER #1172
Regarding 2 Timothy 2:12, it is a difficult verse to understand, but it seems to be speaking to the Christians there in Ephesus where Timothy is the pastor. It is certainly true that if the unsaved *"deny,"* reject, or don't believe in the Lord Jesus Christ, they will go to Hell. But there is *"denial"* that we saved people should be warned about as well. Peter is an example. I don't believe we can lose our salvation once we're saved, but any such *"denials"* in various ways will be like *"hay, wood, and stubble"* at the judgment seat of Christ which things will be burned up by the fire that shall test them (1 Corinthians 3:12-15).

Matthew 8:22-23 speaks of professing Christians who are not possessing Christians. They parade around as Christians, but are only actors and lost, hence bound for Hell.

CHAPTER X
QUESTIONS ABOUT
BIBLE INSPIRATION

King James Bible Not Inspired
QUESTION #1173

I stand firm on the belief that the King James Bible 1611 Authorized Version is both *"inspired and preserved."* It is not accurate to believe that only the Hebrew, Aramaic, and Greek texts were *"inspired."* If God breathed life into the Words He put into His original pages and He promised us that He would not allow these words to pass away until all Scripture was fulfilled, then I beg to differ from you. When you say the King James Bible is not *"inspired,"* you remove its life. After I listened to Daniel S. Waite's streaming video, I was shocked at the suggestion of the belief that the King James Authorized Version is not *"inspired."* Please reconsider your stand and go back to the drawing board and become like a child again and see it in simple terms. It is obvious that you stand by the King James Bible otherwise you wouldn't have given a 400th anniversary conference. You have to see the King James Bible both *"inspired and preserved"* in order to defend it, or you become a *"weak sister"*!

ANSWER #1173

For you to believe that any translation of God's own inspired and inerrant Words in Hebrew, Aramaic, and Greek can also be truthfully considered as *"inspired,"* you will have to make it up out of your own brain as Peter Ruckman, Gail Riplinger, and their followers have done. You have no authority whatsoever to label a translation (even the King James Bible) as being *"inspired"* or *"God-breathed."* The only New Testament Bible verse we have that speaks of "inspiration" is found in 2 Timothy 3:16:

2 Timothy 3:16

*"All **scripture is given by inspiration of God**, and is profitable for doctrine, for reproof, for correction, for instruction in righteousness:"*

The only thing that is mentioned that is said to be *"given by inspiration of God"* and THEOPNEUSTOS (*"God-breathed"*) is *"all scripture."* The Greek Word for *"scripture"* here is GRAPHE. To determine the meaning of the word, GRAPHE, you must look at all of its uses found in the New Testament. If my search is correct, I found a total of 51 uses of this word, GRAPHE. In every one of these references, the word, GRAPHE, refers either to a Hebrew Old Testament verse or to a Greek New Testament verse. Therefore, Biblically speaking, that which has been *"given by inspiration of God"* must be totally, uniquely, solely, and exclusively to either Hebrew, Aramaic, or Greek Words. Conversely, *"inspiration"* in any form whatsoever used to describe the King James Bible, or any other translation is totally out of line, unbiblical, and therefore heretical. As all true doctrine, so this doctrine of *"inspiration"* must be based upon the clear teachings of the Bible rather than on the false assumptions and speculations of men or women.

King James Bible Inspiration

QUESTION #1174

Since the last time I wrote to you, I have considered matters before God, and have studied the matter of the inspiration of the King James Bible further. I desire to make this statement of my revised position. While I do not accept that the King James Bible is inspired in the Ruckman sense, I do believe that the King James Bible is inspired because it is clearly a product of God's preservation, and the King James Bible has also been brought about by the will of God working through men selecting the right texts and accurately translating them into English; it is an inspired translation in the English language because it is an accurate translation of the original languages. The involvement of God in the version is evident by the quality, accuracy, and reliability of the translation. I abandon my previous position of maintaining that inspiration can only apply to the original language texts, since it is plain to my understanding now that an accurate translation in English (King James Bible) of an inspired work is as equally inspired as the original. Is my position Biblical?

ANSWER #1174

I do **not** believe your current position is Biblical. Your former position which placed *"inspiration"* solely at the level of God's Hebrew, Aramaic, and Greek Words is the Biblical position. I will answer as I have done in the previous question:

> *"For you to believe that any translation of God's own inspired and inerrant Words in Hebrew, Aramaic, and Greek can also be truthfully considered as "inspired," you will have to make it up out of your own brain as*

Peter Ruckman, Gail Riplinger, and their followers have done. You have no authority whatsoever to label a translation (even the King James Bible) as being "inspired" or "God-breathed." The only New Testament Bible verse we have that speaks of "inspiration" is found in 2 Timothy 3:16:

2 Timothy 3:16
"All <u>scripture is given by inspiration of God</u>, and is profitable for doctrine, for reproof, for correction, for instruction in righteousness:"

> *The only thing that is mentioned that is said to be "given by inspiration of God" and THEOPNEUSTOS ("God-breathed") is "all scripture." The Greek Word for "scripture" here is GRAPHE. To determine the meaning of the word, GRAPHE, you must look at all of its uses found in the New Testament. If my search is correct, I found a total of 50 or 51 uses of this word, GRAPHE. In every one of these references, the word, GRAPHE, refers either to a Hebrew Old Testament verse or to a Greek New Testament verse. Therefore, Biblically speaking, that which has been "given by inspiration of God" must be totally, uniquely, solely, and exclusively to either Hebrew, Aramaic, or Greek Words. Conversely, "inspiration" in any form whatsoever used to describe the King James Bible, or any other translation is totally out of line, unbiblical, and therefore heretical. As all true doctrine, so this doctrine of "inspiration" must be based upon the clear teachings of the Bible rather than on the false assumptions and speculations of men or women."*

What Does "Inspiration" Mean?
QUESTION #1175

The reason I asked you about the "*inspiration*" was because of John MacArthur who said:

> "*the word inspiration comes from the Latin that means breathe-in, while the Greek, Theopneustos, means breathe-out. The word inspiration is not a translation of the Greek word Theopneustos.*"

Do you agree with John MacArthur on this?

ANSWER #1175

I believe John MacArthur is not correct on this. THEOPNEUSTOS was not translated in our King James Bible as "*inspiration*" as MacArthur falsely stated. It was translated by the King James Bible translators with five English words, not one word, "*inspiration*." The five words were "***given by inspiration*** *of God.*" One word for THEOPNEUSTOS might be "*God-breathed*" coming from THEOS and PNEUSTOS (coming from the verb, PNEO "*to breathe.*") All the Words of Hebrew, Aramaic, and Greek were "*breathed out*" by God and then those Words were "*breathed in*" to the human writers. They then wrote them down.

."Inspiration" a Proper Translation?
QUESTION #1176
In 2 Timothy 3:16 it says "*All scripture is given by inspiration.*" In the King James Bible it uses the word "*inspiration.*" Is that a wrong translation?
ANSWER #1176
You gave only part of the translation for THEOPNEUSTOS. In the King James Bible, it is "*given by inspiration of God.*" This Greek adjective (THEOPNEUSTOS) is properly translated by the King James Bible. It is a compound Greek word coming from two Greek words, THEOS ("*God*") and PNEUSTOS which comes from PNEO ("*to breathe*"). Literally, it is "*breathed out by God,*" or "*God-breathed.*" It refers to the original Hebrew, Aramaic, and Greek Words, and not to any translation of those Words in any other language, including the King James Bible in English.

What Do We Call Accurate Copies?
QUESTION #1177
It is very helpful for me to understand the importance of "Why not use '*inspiration*' with the King James Bible?" We would have to re-define "*inspiration*" if it were applied to anything other than the originals. I have been trying to understand better the whole idea of "*inspiration,*" so that I can properly explain or teach my position clearly and effectively. I would like to ask one more question so as I can understand more clearly. Would we consider the Textus Receptus that I bought from the DBS to be "*inspired*"?
ANSWER #1177
I'll answer your question about accurate copies of the original Hebrew, Aramaic, or Greek Words in this way. The **process** of God's breathing-out His Words happened only once as the Lord Jesus Christ gave God the Holy Spirit the Words to impart to the human writers. However, once this **process** had been completed, the **product** of this **process** consisted of Hebrew, Aramaic, and Greek Words. The exact copies of these Words and only the exact copies of those original Words which were given by the **process** of Divine inspiration can be referred to as "*inspired Words,*" even though they did not come into

being by the process of God's breathing them out, but by man's accurate copying of them down through the many centuries.

The second part of your question dealt with the Hebrew, Aramaic, and Greek Words that underlie the King James Bible (such as Scrivener's Greek edition of Beza's 5th edition of 1598). Though I cannot prove it to any one who might disagree with me on it, it is my personal belief, after more than 40 years of studying, thinking, writing, and speaking on this subject, based on both facts and faith, that the Hebrew, Aramaic, and Greek Words underlying the King James Bible are copies of the exact Words of the originals and can therefore be called "*the inspired Words of God*" or "*God-breathed*" Words. I also have, in the King James Bible, the only accurate, faithful, and reliable English translation of those "*inspired Words*" of Hebrew, Aramaic, and Greek which underlie it.

Inspiration Process vs. Product
QUESTION #1178

I have another question that I have been really thinking about for well over a month now. It continues to churn in my head. I have really been struggling with the whole theme of "*inspiration*." I know that we agree that the King James Bible was not "*given by inspiration*," and that only the originals (that being what Moses, Paul, John, Peter, and the other authors physically wrote) were "*given by inspiration*." That "*given by inspiration*" was a one-time act when God breathed-out those Words to the writer who then recorded them for us. However, my question is that if those are copied correctly, faithfully, and accurately then, though they were not "*re-inspired*" when they were copied, they are accurate, faithful copies of those originally "*inspired*" Words thus carrying with them that original "*inspiration*" and thus making them "*inspired Words*." They are not newly "*given by inspiration*," but rather carry with them that original "*inspiration*."

Now when they are translated, and that translation is a very faithful, accurate translation of those originally "*inspired Words*," would not those words then have the same claim to that "*inspiration*"? We understand that they were not "*inspired*" at the time of translation, and were only "*inspired*" at the time they were written down. However, I find it hard to separate the fact that those are the "*inspired Words*" in the original languages (i.e. accurate, faithful, exact copies of the originals), and those Words, when translated, then lose their claim to "*inspiration*" in whatever language they are translated into.

That is my dilemma, and question. Where exactly is the line drawn on a text being considered as an "*inspired*" text? (With the understanding we are not talking about "*given by inspiration*.") This is an honest and sincere question that I'm really struggling with and trying to understand. I certainly don't mean to appear or seem wishy-washy. It is something that I earnestly want to understand and be able to take a firm stand on, without wavering one way or the other. I look forward to your input and appreciate your taking the time to read and respond.

ANSWER #1178

Your question is similar to that asked by others. It really asks the difference between the **PROCESS** of inspiration and the **PRODUCT** of inspiration.

I'll give you the answer I gave another person on this:

> *"I'll answer your question about accurate copies of the original Hebrew, Aramaic, or Greek Words in this way. The process of God's breathing-out His Words happened only once as the Lord Jesus Christ gave God the Holy Spirit the Words to impart to the human writers. However, once this process had been completed, the product of this process consisted of Hebrew, Aramaic, and Greek Words. The exact copies of these Words, and only the exact copies of those original Words which were given by the process of Divine inspiration can be referred to as "inspired Words," even though they did not come into being by the process of God's breathing them out, but by man's accurate copying of them down through the many centuries."*

The KJB Not "Given By Inspiration"

QUESTION #1179

Do you believe the King James Bible was *"given by inspiration of God"*?

ANSWER #1179

No. The only Words that were *"given by inspiration of God"* were the Words that God Himself gave us in the original, preserved, and inerrant Hebrew, Aramaic, and Greek Words which underlie the King James Bible. As our Dean Burgon Society has written in its yearly questionnaire for all its leaders to sign, these underlying Words **alone** can be called by any of these five terms: (1) *"given by inspiration of God,"* (2) *"God-breathed,"* (3) *"inspired of God,"* (4) *"verbally inspired,"* or (5) *"inspired."* None of these terms should be used for the King James Bible. The term (5) "inspired" cannot be used of the King James Bible in any sense at all, including *"derivative inspiration,"* *"indirect inspiration,"* *"having the mark of inspiration,"* *"inspired in a 'generic'* *or general sense*" or any other similar terms that might be brought up to modify "*inspired*" or "*inspiration*." Some people say they don't believe the King James Bible is "*inspired,*" yet they use some of these four descriptive phrases with the word "*inspired*." This is unscriptural. I believe that the King James Bible can be described as the only "*true*," "*faithful*," and "*accurate*" English translation of its underlying Hebrew, Aramaic, and Greek Words.

CHAPTER XI
QUESTIONS ABOUT
DISPENSATIONALISM

O.T. Feast Days for the N.T.?
QUESTION #1180

How would I refute a teaching that says the Feast Days of the Old Testament are for today's Church?

ANSWER #1180

Here are a few verses to use in this area. I wouldn't waste my time arguing with people who want to keep Old Testament feast days because they probably won't change. But they are totally wrong. The law of Moses, where those days were enjoined, is no longer any part whatsoever for the born-again Christian in the New Testament under God's grace. The "Jews for Jesus" group is one of the groups that err in this practice, but there's no stopping them. They are hostile to any correction in these areas, sad to say. The dispensational approach to the Bible makes these things very clear. Here are some Bible verses to show we are not under any part of the Law of Moses in this dispensation of grace:

Romans 6:14–15

"14 For sin shall not have dominion over you: for ye are not under the law, but under grace. 15 What then? shall we sin, because we are not under the law, but under grace? God forbid."

Galatians 4:9–11

"9 But now, after that ye have known God, or rather are known of God, how turn ye again to the weak and beggarly elements, whereunto ye desire again to be in bondage? 10 Ye observe days, and months, and times, and years. 11 I am afraid of you, lest I have bestowed upon you labour in vain."

Colossians 2:16–17

"*16 Let no man therefore judge you in meat, or in drink, or in respect of an holyday, or of the new moon, or of the sabbath days:* 17 Which are <u>*a shadow*</u> *of things to come; but the body is of Christ.*"

The Purpose of Dispensationalism
QUESTION #1181
I have a sincere question. What is dispensationalism for?
ANSWER #1181
Dispensationalism is to enable us to understand the entire sixty-six Old Testament and New Testament books of the Bible. It shows clearly that God gave different commands and rules of life to different groups of mankind at different periods of time in the Bible. I recommend that you get my *Outline of Dispensationalism* (**BFT #3078, 30 pages @ $6.00 + $3.00 S&H**). This will tell you the purpose and need for understanding the Bible with a dispensational understanding of it.

Explaining Dispensationalism Briefly
QUESTION #1182
I think I understand how dispensationalism works and the time lines. But I've never understood what it is for. In other words, what is the purpose of this system of theology? Is this something you can answer in a paragraph?
ANSWER #1182
The purpose of dispensationalism is to be able to understand the meaning of the entire Bible. God had different responsibilities for mankind at different periods or dispensations of time. We cannot understand the Bible clearly without such a dispensational approach. For example, God did not tell us not to eat of the tree in the garden of Eden. He told it to Adam and Eve in a different dispensation. God did not tell us to build an ark to save mankind, but He told this to Noah. He did not give a promise to us that he would make of us a great nation as He did to Abraham. He did not give us the ten commandments, the sacrificial system, and the social laws of Moses, but He did to Moses. We are not under any obligation of that dispensation. He gave us the gospel of the Lord Jesus Christ throughout this dispensation of grace based on the shedding of His blood and His death on the cross of Calvary which was never given to any of the previous dispensations. The rule of the Lord Jesus

Christ during the millennium has never happened in any of the other dispensations either. It is possible that there are trans-dispensational truths that go throughout the dispensations, but usually man's responsibilities are different in different dispensations.

Hyper-Dispensationalism Refuted
QUESTION #1183
I am reading a book by Douglas Stauffer that sounds dispensational. He says that the epistles of Hebrews, Peter, James, John, and Revelation have not any message for the church age, only Paul's epistles are for the church. What is your judgment on this?

ANSWER #1183
This is from what is known as a "hyper-dispensational" source. This group of people wrongly accepts only the letters of Paul for this age and none of the other epistles. I believe this is a heresy. Under the dispensation and age of grace in which we are now living, all the books that were written after the Lord Jesus Christ died on the cross (and after the Holy Spirit came upon the Christians on the day of Pentecost, and the Church which is Christ's Body was established) are both to us and for us. The Old Testament books, and the books written about the activities before the beginning of the Church which is Christ's Body though not written to us, are nevertheless *"for our learning"* as Romans 15:4 states:

> *"For whatsoever things were written aforetime were written **for our learning**, that we through patience and comfort of the scriptures might have hope."*

Hyper-Dispensationalist Groups
QUESTION #1184
Further to our phone conversation earlier today, I would appreciate your comments on the following that I have cut from Mr. Stanford's website. It would seem that he would not be a Hyper-Dispensationalist. Upon thinking of some of the points you made that would be "Hyper" Dispensational, I remembered reading that Mr. Stanford did not hold those views, so I went to his website to see if he had been accused of being hyper-dispensational and indeed he had. What is your view of his position?

ANSWER #1184
1.   Your quotations were a good summary of the four positions of when the church began: (1) Acts 2; (2) Acts 9; (3) Acts 13, or (4) Acts 28. Some put the beginning of the church at John the Baptist or Christ.

2.   Though Stanford disavows Acts 9, 13, or 28 beginnings of the Church (which is fine), he wants to exalt *"God's revelation to Paul"* which I think means, lesser revelations to other parts of the New Testament such as the books of James, 1 & 2 Peter, 1 & 2 & 3 John, Jude, and Revelation. In other words, Stanford is not an extreme dispensationalist, but his possible pushing of Paul's writings more than the others books mentioned above leaves some questions in my mind. I believe this is a false and heretical position of Bible interpretation. Historic dispensational interpretation of the Bible, yes. But hyper-dispensationalism of any of the four kinds, no.

CHAPTER XII
QUESTIONS ABOUT
THE SPANISH BIBLE

Is There a Faithful Spanish Bible?

QUESTION #1185

Is there a Spanish version of the King James Bible that is faithful? Would this be possible to do in a language other than English and still maintain the fidelity of the King James Bible? Why is the letter from the translators of the King James Bible to the reader no longer printed in front of our King James Bible? Do you feel it would be advantageous to own an original 1611 King James Bible?

ANSWER #1185

I believe that the most faithful Spanish Bible to the underlying Hebrew, Aramaic, and Greek Words is the one by Dr. Humberto Gomez, the Reina/Valera/Gomez. We carry it. The King James Bible's Preface *"To the Reader"* is long and therefore is not carried in most King James Bibles. I think our *Defined King James Bible* is good enough. You don't need the original 1611 which has different spellings, etc. Nelson publishers has this edition in print if you want to get a copy.

John 1:1–"Verbo" vs. "Palabra"
QUESTION #1186

Much is being said about our usage in our Spanish Bible of the word *"verbo"* for *"Word"* in John 1:1, rather than *"palabra."* The criticism is coming from Gail Riplinger, who defends the Monterrey Bible. She implies that our Bible is corrupt for this matter. Without elaborating on Gail Riplinger herself, do you have an opinion regarding the use of *"Verbo"* rather than *"Palabra"*?

ANSWER #1186

I memorized John 1:1 ("*In the beginning was the __Word__*") in Spanish from the Spanish New Testament many years ago. I see no reason to change the word "*verbo*" for "*palabra*." Gail Riplinger's Spanish Bible idol, the Monterrey Bible, was drawn up by an Anglo whose mother tongue is English, not Spanish. In his Spanish translation, Bill Parks, though true to the Textus Receptus in most places, has made many changes not required to be faithful to the Textus Receptus. They are only changes for the sake of change. They are not needed, or warranted, and, in some cases, are incorrect translations. I don't know the detailed history of the Spanish words "*verbo*" and "*palabra*." However, when an English-speaking translator who is not a Spanish speaking national wants to change the time-honored word, "*verbo*" for something else, I would personally reject that change.

Daniel 3:25 and Luke 2:22

QUESTION #1187

I just received an email today from an Hispanic Pastor that I know personally here in Puerto Rico. He uses the Reina-Valera 1960 version. I believe he is even in favor of the Critical Texts. He brought up a discussion on Daniel 3:25 and Luke 2:22. I am working on a response to him but there were a couple items he brought up that I would like to see your comment on.

1. Concerning Luke 2:22, he claims that the TR text of Scrivener (which the DBS prints) actually agrees with the Critical Texts and all the corrupted English Bibles and also the Spanish 1960 in saying "*their purification*" rather than "*her purification*" as the King James Bible and our Reina/Valera/Gomez reads. Can you verify if this is true or not?

2. Concerning Daniel 3:25, he claims that "*a son of __the__ gods*" is more correct than "*the Son of God*" because it is actually a more literal translation of the underlying Hebrew text. Can you verify if that is true or not?

ANSWER #1187

1.   Luke 2:22.   Your friend is dead wrong on Luke 2:22. Dr. Frederick Scrivener's Greek (which both the Trinitarian Bible Society and the Dean Burgon Society have reprinted) and all the Received Texts that I know about are clear on using the word, "*her*" purification. Only the Gnostic Critical Greek Texts use "*their*" purification which is rank heresy. I wonder where your friend got this erroneous idea?

2.   Daniel 3:25.   The words are not in Hebrew, but are in Aramaic, BAR ELOHIN, ("*son of God*") even if ELOHIN might be plural, like the

Hebrew ELOHIM, it is taken as a collective and translated as GOD rather than GODS.   Furthermore, there is no article (like our English,"*the*") before ELOHIN, so how could they put in "*a son of the gods*"? Your friend should stay with the King James Bible and the Reina/Valera/Gomez and their readings.

CHAPTER XIII
QUESTIONS ABOUT THE
BIBLE'S PRESERVATION

Bible Preservation and the KJB
QUESTION #1188
I sent a friend an article entitled "*A plea for a Perfect Bible*" by Dr. Jeffrey Khoo. Where is that "*perfect Bible*?" Does he refer to the King James Bible?
ANSWER #1188
This is an article on Bible preservation. The doctrine of Bible preservation is concerned, not with any of the many translations of the Bible (including the King James Bible), but refers exclusively to the original and preserved Hebrew, Aramaic, and Greek Words underlying the King James Bible. The King James Bible has translated accurately and reliably into English these inspired and preserved Hebrew, Aramaic, and Greek Words.

I believe that God's providential preservation of the Scriptures concerns not only the doctrines, but also the very Hebrew, Aramaic, and Greek Words of the Old and New Testaments, right down to the last "*jot and tittle*" (See Psalm 12:6-7; Matthew 5:18; 24:35; Mark 13:31; Luke 21:33; and Revelation 22:18-19). Then God's original and preserved Hebrew, Aramaic, and Greek Words (to the last "*jot and tittle*") were accurately translated for us in the King James Bible.

Documentation on Preservation
QUESTION #1189
I've stopped using the Dead sea scrolls. I know I should use the Masoretic Hebrew text for the Old Testament. Can you direct me to a good book or online article that isn't too complicated that I can read and use to prove that the Bible has not been changed? Also are there any books or articles dealing with how the New Testament has not been changed or corrupted?

ANSWER #1189

For the answers to these questions, I would recommend my book, *Defending The King James Bible* (BFT #1594 @ $12.00 + $8.00 S&H). In Chapter Two, the Hebrew, Aramaic, and Greek Words are shown to be preserved accurately by the Lord. This is a good beginning chapter on the subject of Bible preservation. In the back of this book, there are other books and articles on this theme that are listed.

The Bible's Words Preserved

QUESTION #1190

I am working on an article, and need your opinion. Did Jesus, who is the *"Word made flesh"* (John 1:1), speak His own words, or the words of His Father? Is there a difference? Was Christ more of a *"messenger"* than the Author of God's Words?

ANSWER #1190

Sometimes the Lord Jesus Christ gave His Words, and sometimes the Lord Jesus Christ gave the Words of His Father. Here are some verses on it.

Matthew 24:35
"Heaven and earth shall pass away, but __my words__ shall not pass away."

Mark 8:38
"Whosoever therefore shall be ashamed __of me and of my words__ in this adulterous and sinful generation; of him also shall the Son of man be ashamed, when he cometh in the glory of his Father with the holy angels."

Mark 13:31
"Heaven and earth shall pass away: but __my words__ shall not pass away."

John 14:23–24
"Jesus answered and said unto him, If a man love me, he will keep __my words__: and my Father will love him, and we will come unto him, and make our abode with him. He that loveth me not keepeth not __my sayings__: and __the word__ which ye hear is __not mine__, but __the Father's__ which sent me."

John 17:8

*"For I have given unto them **the words** which **thou gavest me**; and they have received them, and have known surely that I came out from thee, and they have believed that thou didst send me."*

The following verses show how the Lord Jesus Christ is the Author of all the Words of the New Testament which were written after He went Home to Heaven.

John 16:12-15

*"12 **I have yet many things to say unto you**, but ye cannot bear them now. 13 Howbeit when he, the Spirit of truth, is come, he will guide you into all truth: for he shall not speak of himself; but **whatsoever he shall hear**, that shall he speak: and he will shew you things to come. 14 He shall glorify me: for **he shall receive of mine, and shall shew it unto you**. 15 All things that the Father hath are mine: therefore said I, that **he shall take of mine, and shall shew it unto you**."*

Bible Preservation

QUESTION #1191

I have a question about the preservation of early manuscripts. I know that modern version advocates voice their support of the "oldest and best." I understand that you and others explain that the Vaticanus and Sinaiticus are the oldest and were preserved because they weren't in active use. Which would be one more support in favor that they were corrupt and not used by faithful Bible-believers. That makes sense to me. The "oldest manuscript" Bible critic crowd have one more leg knocked out from under them when you say that B and aleph aren't even the oldest manuscripts. There's Peshitta and other manuscripts which are dated 100-200 AD which agree with the TR.

ANSWER #1191

You are right by saying that Vatican and Sinai are not the oldest manuscripts. There are many that are earlier than 350 A.D. or so, which is the approximate dates of both the Vatican and the Sinai. Though the **materials** on which Vatican and Sinai are written are older than the materials on which the Textus Receptus manuscripts are written, the **words** on these Textus Receptus manuscripts are much older than those of the Vatican and Sinai, going back to the Apostolic age itself. I have shown this by various means in my meetings in defense of the Textus Receptus and the King James Bible.

CHAPTER XIV
QUESTIONS ABOUT NINE
MISCELLANEOUS TOPICS

1. Meaning of Summa Cum Laude

QUESTION #1192

What does *"summa cum laude"* mean?

ANSWER #1192

It is Latin for *"with highest honor."* Many schools and colleges confer three levels of Latin honors, although some do not use the third, namely: (1) *"cum laude,"* meaning *"with honor";* (2) *"magna cum laude,"* meaning *"with great or high honor,"* and (3) *"summa cum laude,"* meaning *"with highest honor."*

2. Floyd Jones' Bible Version Book

QUESTION #1193

What do you think of this book, *Which Version Is The Bible?* by Floyd Nolen Jones, Th.D., Ph.D.? The book is on the LINK below:
http://www.3bible.com/books/Which%20Version%20is%20the%20Bible.pdf

ANSWER #1193

Dr. Jones stands for the King James Bible. He does a very good job in his support of it. His documentation is clear and can be followed easily. It is a good book. Our Bible For Today ministry carries this book.

3. Various Books to Recommend

QUESTION #1194

I have six questions to ask you. I hope you will be able to give me brief answers to all of them.

1.   Which Lexicon do you recommend that remains true to the Textus Receptus?

2.   What is your opinion on *Jay Green's Interlinear New Testament*? What are some of the weakness and strengths? I own it but have only used it a few times.

3.   Which concordance (if any) do you recommend? I own an updated *Strong's Exhaustive Concordance* and want to ensure it is the best available option.

4.   Which *Systematic Theology* series do you recommend that best represents our Independent Fundamental King James Bible views? Dr. Lewis Sperry Chafer's? I own Ryrie, Thiessen (Moderate) and Hodge (Reformed).

5.   Is there a commentary set that you would recommend? I know that you have commented on several books of the Bible. Maybe you have a complete set? I own Matthew Henry, Jamieson, Fausset, and Brown, and J. Vernon McGee.

6.   Will you be teaching any Greek classes soon? Being local, I would be very interested. Please let me know.

ANSWER #1194

Here are my brief answers to your six questions that you have asked.

1.   I recommend the *Analytical Hebrew Lexicon* and the *Analytical Greek Lexicon*. These can be ordered through the Bible For Today and can be drop-shipped from the publisher. They are about $25 or $30 each.

2.   Jay Green uses the Beza's Greek 5th edition 1598 text which is good, but he uses his own King James Bible-2 rather than the King James Bible in the margins. Though he might not have always accurate English translations for the Greek or Hebrew Words, at least you can tell which Hebrew or Greek Word is being used and can look them up yourself in one of the above lexicons.

3.   *Strong's Concordance* is useful. In this concordance, you can get the Hebrew or Greek Word used and look it up in the lexicons above for further meanings.

4.   I was taught at Dallas Seminary by Dr. Chafer himself. We used his 8-volume theology. Though he gives a Presbyterian viewpoint in many places (which I do not fully agree with), his dispensational and premillennial understanding of the Bible is excellent. Now, all 8-volumes have been combined into 4 large volumes. Our son, Pastor Daniel Waite, taught it over the Internet to his theology classes. These classes can be seen on the Internet by clicking on this LINK: http://biblefortoday.org/chafers.htm

5.   The *Bethany Parallel Commentary* gives many of the old-time Bible teachers and their comments in the Old and New Testaments. They were uncontaminated by the new Bible versions. Most of them used the King James Bible.

6.   I suggest you take our Internet Greek course that I taught many years ago.   You can see it (with the *Hershey Davis's* Greek textbook) at BibleForToday.org   You can see http://www.biblefortoday.org/greek.htm for the direct link for the first year Greek course.

4. Dealing with Demons
QUESTION #1195

1.   I would like to discuss with you (or maybe hear in a sermon) why you believe a Christian cannot be possessed by a demon. Why else would Peter curse Jesus if the Devil had not gotten hold of him?

2.   Are we to cast out demons? If so, from whom?

3.   Why does it say some demons only come out *"through prayer and fasting"*?

Matthew 17:19-21

*"Then came the disciples to Jesus apart, and said, **Why could not we cast him out**? And Jesus said unto them, Because of your unbelief: for verily I say unto you, **If ye have faith** as a grain of mustard seed, ye shall say unto this mountain, Remove hence to yonder place; and it shall remove; and nothing shall be impossible unto you. Howbeit **this kind goeth not out but by prayer and fasting**."*

ANSWER #1195

1.   I do not believe that born-again Christians can be demon-possessed because God the Holy Spirit indwells them. They can be demon-influenced, however. This is what happened to Peter in the instance you speak of (Matthew 16:21-23).

2.   I do not believe the special apostolic power of casting out demons ["*devils*," KJB] has been preserved in this age of grace. This power ceased, along with all the other so-called sign gifts when the Bible was completed in 90 or 100 A.D.

3.   As in Matthew 17:19-21 quoted above, though these apostles had the special gift and power, they lacked faith to do this. They were rebuked by the Lord Jesus Christ because of this lack of faith.

5. More on Demon Possession
QUESTION #1196

Can you have demons without demon possession? Wouldn't *"possession"* mean you would have no use of your faculties like the two men in the tombs in the country of the Gergesenes?

Matthew 8:28-29

*"And when he was come to the other side into the country of the Gergesenes, there met him **two possessed with devils, coming out of the tombs**, exceeding fierce, so that no man might pass by that way. And, behold, they cried out, saying, What have we to do with thee, Jesus, thou Son of God? art thou come hither to torment us before the time?"*

ANSWER #1196

Though it is possible for unsaved non-Christian people to be possessed by demons [*"devils,"* KJB], I do not believe a born-again Christian can be possessed by demons [*"devils,"* KJB]. The saved Christians have God the Holy Spirit indwelling them. Therefore, demons [*"devils,"* KJB] cannot indwell them along side of God the Holy Spirit. However, it is possible for the born-again Christian to be **influenced** (though not possessed) by demons [*"devils,"* KJB] if they are not walking in the power of the Holy Spirit. This was the case with Peter when he denied the predictive words of the Lord Jesus Christ.

Matthew 16:21-23

*"From that time forth began Jesus to shew unto his disciples, how that **he must go unto Jerusalem, and suffer many things** of the elders and chief priests and scribes, and be killed, and be raised again the third day. Then **Peter took him, and began to rebuke him, saying, Be it far from thee, Lord: this shall not be unto thee**. But he turned, and said unto Peter, **Get thee behind me, Satan**: thou art an offence unto me: for thou savourest not the things that be of God, but those that be of men."*

Peter, an apostle of the Lord Jesus Christ was being influenced by Satan in his denial of the Lord Jesus Christ's predictive words.

6. The Black Robe Regiment

QUESTION #1197

I have a question regarding the "Black Robe Regiment." In my research I have discovered that this group is an ecumenical group of pastors and lay leaders who are joining up to save America and the Constitution. My growing concern is how the Evangelical Churches (even the non-501 c (3) churches) are joining up with this movement. There are several sites online that pastors can join. Glenn Beck and David Barton have the main ones. Do you know about this group? Are you supportive of this movement?

ANSWER #1197
I agree with you in being against religious ecumenism of any kind. If Glenn Beck and David Barton are for this, I must stand completely against it. Both Beck and Barton are comfortable in merging Roman Catholicism, Judaism, Mormonism, Masons, liberal Protestantism, and even some evangelical Protestantism into one huge ecumenical mess which is contrary to the Words of God.

7. The Dean Burgon Society

QUESTION #1198
Is Emmanuel Baptist Theological Seminary in Newington, CT in agreement with the Dean Burgon Society? I really enjoyed reading and studying Dr. Kulus' book *Those So-Called Errors* which is endorsed by Emmanuel and Dr. Thomas Strouse. I found it quite helpful in understanding certain passages of Scripture.

ANSWER #1198
The Emanuel Baptist Theological Seminary in Newington, CT has made a number of changes in recent years both in the faculty and in the pastor of the sponsoring church. In a recent call to the school, I was informed that the seminary is no longer in operation. All I can tell you is about the former position in regard to the Articles of Faith of the Dean Burgon Society (DBS). In past years, they opposed the DBS since it was a *"para-church"* organization instead of one sponsored by a local church. Another former difference was their insistence that only certain kinds of local Baptist Churches make up the *"body of Christ"* rather than all born-again Christians of whatever church or denomination they belong to. The DBS Articles of Faith states:

"I. Spiritual Unity: We believe in the real spiritual unity in Christ of all redeemed by His precious blood."

If only certain kinds of Baptists make up the Body of Christ, this destroys the *"spiritual unity."* The book by Dr. Kulus is a good book. I agree he has done a very good job in this book.

8. Baptist Mid Missions and DBS

QUESTION #1199
Are you familiar with the Bible Society of Baptist Mid Missions? Are they one of the Bible translators that the Dean Burgon Society would recommend? Thank you (Isaiah 40:8).

ANSWER #1199

The Dean Burgon Society and the Bible For Today ministries would not recommend Bibles International of the Baptist Mid-Missions because they do not believe that they should use exclusively the Received Text Hebrew, Aramaic, and Greek Words underlying the King James Bible as the basis for all foreign language translations. They sometimes use the so-called "Majority" text which differs from that underlying the King James Bible in 1500 to 1800 places. I am not certain either that every one of those connected with the Baptist Mid-Missions uses and defends the King James Bible and the Hebrew, Aramaic, and Greek Words underlying it. In fact, I am certain that many of them (if not all of them) favor modern versions such as the NIV, NASV, ESV, NKJV, etc.

9. HIV And AIDS

QUESTION #1200

What are the dangers of the HIV virus and AIDS? How are these transmitted to others?

ANSWER #1200

The following answer was sent to me from a medical doctor who is a born-again Christian. I wanted our readers to have his answer.

HIV Information:

HIV infection leads to AIDS (acquired immune deficiency syndrome), which is the final stage of HIV disease.

Here is how HIV is spread:

HIV has been found in saliva, tears, nervous system tissue, spinal fluid, blood, semen (including pre-seminal fluid, which is the liquid that comes out before ejaculation), vaginal fluid, and breast milk. However, only blood, semen, vaginal secretions, and breast milk generally transmit infection to others.

The virus can be spread (transmitted):

Through sexual contact -- including oral, vaginal, and anal sex.

Through blood--via blood transfusions (now extremely rare in the U.S.) or needle sharing.

From mother to child -- a pregnant woman can transmit the virus to her fetus through their shared blood circulation, or a nursing mother can transmit it to her baby in her breast milk.

Other methods of spreading the virus are rare and include accidental needle injury, artificial insemination with infected donated semen, and organ transplantation with infected organs.

HIV infection is NOT spread by:

Casual contact such as hugging

Mosquitoes

Participation in sports

Touching items previously touched by a person infected with the virus

AIDS and blood or organ donation:

AIDS is NOT transmitted to a person who DONATES blood or organs. Those who donate organs are never in direct contact with those who receive them. Likewise, a person who donates blood is not in contact with the person receiving it. In all these procedures, sterile needles and instruments are used.

However, HIV can be transmitted to a person RECEIVING blood or organs from an infected donor. To reduce this risk, blood banks and organ donor programs screen donors, blood, and tissues thoroughly.

People at highest risk for getting HIV include:

Injection drug users who share needles.

Infants born to mothers with HIV who didn't receive HIV therapy during pregnancy.

People engaging in unprotected sex, especially with people who have other high-risk behaviors, are HIV-positive, or have AIDS.

People who received blood transfusions or clotting products between 1977 and 1985 (before screening for the virus became standard practice).

Sexual partners of those who participate in high-risk activities (such as injection drug use or anal sex).

Index of Words and Phrases

About the Author

The author of this book, Dr. D. A. Waite, received a B.A. (Bachelor of Arts) in classical Greek and Latin from the University of Michigan in 1948, a Th.M. (Master of Theology), with high honors, in New Testament Greek Literature and Exegesis from Dallas Theological Seminary in 1952, an M.A. (Master of Arts) in Speech from Southern Methodist University in 1953, a Th.D. (Doctor of Theology), with honors, in Bible Exposition from Dallas Theological Seminary in 1955, and a Ph.D. in Speech from Purdue University in 1961. He holds both New Jersey and Pennsylvania teacher certificates in Greek and Language Arts.

He has been a teacher in the areas of Greek, Hebrew, Bible, Speech, and English for over thirty-five years in ten schools, including one junior high, one senior high, four Bible institutes, two colleges, two universities, and one seminary. He served his country as a Navy Chaplain for five years on active duty; pastored three churches; was Chairman and Director of the Radio and Audio-Film Commission of the American Council of Christian Churches; since 1969, has been Founder, President, and Director of THE BIBLE FOR TODAY; since 1978, has been President of the DEAN BURGON SOCIETY; has produced over 800 other studies, books, audio cassettes, CD's, VCR's, or DVD's on various topics; and is heard on a thirty-minute weekly program, IN DEFENSE OF TRADITIONAL BIBLE TEXTS, on radio, and streaming on the Internet at BibleForToday.org, 24/7/365.

Dr. and Mrs. Waite have been married since 1948; they have four sons, one daughter, and, at present, eight grand-children, and eleven great-grandchildren. Since October 4, 1998, he has been the Pastor of the Bible For Today Baptist Church in Collingswood, New Jersey.

Order Blank (p. 1)

Name:_____

Address:_____

City & State:_____Zip:_____

Credit Card #:_____Expires:_____

Latest Books

[ ] Send The Sixth 200 Questions Answered By Dr. D. A. Waite
(188 pp. perfect bound $15.00 + $7.00 S&H)

[ ] Send The Fifth 200 Questions Answered By Dr. D. A. Waite
(150 pp. perfect bound $15.00 + $7.00 S&H)

[ ] Send *The Fourth 200 Questions Answered* By Dr. D. A. Waite
(168 pp. perfect bound $15.00 + $7.00 S&H)

[ ] Send *The Third 200 Questions Answered* By Dr. D. A. Waite
(180 pp. perfect bound $15.00 + $7.00 S&H)

[ ] Send *The Second 200 Questions Answered* By Dr. D. A. Waite
(178 pp. perfect bound $15.00 + $7.00 S&H)

[ ] Send *The First 200 Questions Answered By Dr. D. A. Waite*
(184 pp. perfect bound $12.00 + $7.00 S&H)

[ ] Send *A Critical Answer to James Price's King James Only-
ism* By Pastor D. A. Waite, 184pp, perfect bound ($11+$7 S&H)

[ ] Send *The KJB's Superior Hebrew & Greek Words* by Pastor
D. A. Waite, 104 pp., perfect bound ($10+$7 S&H)

[ ] Send *Soulwinning's Versions-Perversions* by Pastor D. A.
Waite, booklet, 28 pp. ($6+$5 S&H) fully indexed

[ ] Send *2 Timothy—Preaching Verse by Verse*, by Pastor D. A.
Waite, 250 pages, perfect bound ($11+$7 S&H) fully indexed.

[ ] Send *A Critical Answer to God's Word Preserved* by Pastor D.
A. Waite, 192 pp. perfect bound ($11.00+$7.00 S&H)

[ ] Send *Daily Bible Blessings* By Yvonne Waite ($20.00+$8 S&H

[ ] Send *Revelation—Preaching Verse By Verse* By Dr. A. A. Waite
($50+$10 S&H—1030 pages.

Send or Call Orders to:
THE BIBLE FOR TODAY
900 Park Ave., Collingswood, NJ 08108
Phone: 856-854-4452; FAX:--2464; Orders: 1-800 JOHN 10:9
E-Mail Orders: BFT@BibleForToday.org; Credit Cards OK

Order Blank (p. 2)

Name:_____

Address:_____

City & State:_____Zip:_____

Credit Card #:_____Expires:_____

[ ] Send *The Occult Connections of Gail Riplinger* by Dr. Phil
Stringer ($12.00 + $7.00 S&H).

[ ] Send *A WARNING!! On Gail Riplinger's KJB & Multiple
Inspiration HERESY*,133 pp. by Pastor DAW ($12+$7S&H)

[ ] Send *Who Is Gail Riplinger?* 146 pp. by Aleithia O'Brien
($12.00 + $7.00)

[ ] *The Messianic Claims Of Gail A. Riplinger*, By Dr. Phil
Stringer, 108 pp., perfect bound ($12.00 + $7.00 S&H)

[ ] Send Husband-Loving Lessons, by Yvonne S. Waite; $25 +
$7.00 S&H A very valuable marriage manual

[ ] Send *8,000 Differences Between Textus Receptus & Critical
Text* by Dr.J.A. Moorman, 544 pp., hd.back ($20+$7 S&H)

[ ] *Early Manuscripts, Church Fathers, & the Authorized
Version* by Dr. Jack Moorman, $20+$7 S&H. Hardback

[ ] Send *The LIE That Changed the Modern World* by Dr.
H. D. Williams ($16+$7 S&H) Hardback book

[ ] Send *With Tears in My Heart* by Gertrude G. Sanborn.
Hardback 414 pp. ($25+$7 S&H) 400 Christian Poems

Preaching Verse by Verse Books

[ ] Send *2 Timothy—Preaching Verse by Verse*, by Pastor D. A.
Waite, 250 pages, hardback ($11+$7 S&H) fully indexed.

[ ] Send *1 Timothy—Preaching Verse by Verse*, by Pastor D.
A.Waite, 288 pages, hardback ($14+$7 S&H) fully indexed.

More Preaching Verse by Verse Books

[ ] Send *Romans—Preaching Verse by Verse* by Pastor D. A.
Waite 736 pp. Hardback ($25+$7 S&H) fully indexed

Send or Call Orders to:
THE BIBLE FOR TODAY
900 Park Ave., Collingswood, NJ 08108

Phone: 856-854-4452; FAX:—2464; Orders: 1-800 JOHN 10:9
E-Mail Orders: BFT@BibleForToday.org; Credit Cards OK

Order Blank (p. 3)

Name:_____

Address:_____

City & State:_____Zip:_____

Credit Card #:_____Expires:_____

[ ] Send *Colossians & Philemon—Preaching Verse by Verse* by
      Pastor D. A. Waite ($12+$7 S&H) hardback, 240 pages
[ ] Send *First Peter--Preaching Verse By Verse* by Pastor D.
      A. Waite ($10+$7 S&H) hardback, 176 pages
[ ] Send *Philippians--Preaching Verse by Verse* by Pastor D.
      A. Waite ($10+$7 S&H) hardback, 176 pages
[ ] Send *Ephesians--Preaching Verse by Verse* by Pastor D. A.
      Waite ($12+$7 S&H) hardback, 224 pages
[ ] Send *Galatians--Preaching Verse By Verse* by Pastor D. A.
      Waite ($13+$7 S&H) hardback, 216 pages

Books on Bible Texts & Translations

[ ] Send *Defending the King James Bible* by DAW ($12+$7
      S&H) A hardback book, indexed with study questions
[ ] Send *BJU's Errors on Bible Preservation* by Dr. D. A.
      Waite, 110 pages, paperback ($8+$7 S&H) fully indexed
[ ] Send *Fundamentalist Deception on Bible Preservation* by
      Dr.Waite, ($8+$4 S&H), paperback, fully indexed
[ ] Send *Fundamentalist MIS-INFORMATION on Bible Ver-
      sions* by Dr. Waite ($7+$5 S&H) perfect bound, 136 pages
[ ] Send *Fundamentalist Distortions on Bible Versions* by
Dr.Waite ($7+$4 S&H) A perfect bound book, 80 pages
[ ] Send *Fuzzy Facts From Fundamentalists* by Dr. D. A.
      Waite ($8.00 + $7.00 S&H)

More Books on Bible Texts & Translations

[ ] Send *Foes of the King James Bible Refuted* by DAW ($9
      +$7 S&H) A perfect bound book, 164 pages in length
[ ] Send *Central Seminary Refuted on Bible Versions* by Dr.
      Waite ($10+$7 S&H) A perfect bound book, 184 pages
Send or Call Orders to:
THE BIBLE FOR TODAY
900 Park Ave., Collingswood, NJ 08108
Phone: 856-854-4452; FAX:--2464; Orders: 1-800 JOHN 10:9
E-Mail Orders: BFT@BibleForToday.org; Credit Cards OK

Order Blank (p. 4)

Name:_____

Address:_____
0
City & State:_____Zip:_____

Credit Card #:_____Expires:_____
[ ] Send *The Case for the King James Bible* by DAW ($8
+$5 S&H) A perfect bound book, 112 pages in length
[ ] Send *Theological Heresies of Westcott and Hort* by Dr. D.
A. Waite, ($8+$5 S&H) A printed booklet
[ ] Send *Westcott's Denial of Resurrection*, Dr. Waite ($8+$5)
[ ] Send *Four Reasons for Defending KJB* by DAW ($4+$3)

More Books on Texts & Translations

[ ] Send *Holes in the Holman Christian Standard Bible* by Dr.
Waite ($6+$4 S&H) A printed booklet, 40 pages
[ ] Send *Contemporary Eng. Version Exposed*, DAW ($6+$4)
[ ] Send *NIV Inclusive Language Exposed* by DAW ($7+$5)
[ ] Send *24 Hours of KJB Seminar* (4 DVD's) by DAW ($50.00)
+ $10.00 S&H

Books By Dr. Jack Moorman

[ ] Send **Manuscript Digest of the N.T.** (721 pp.) By Dr. Jack
Moorman, copy-machine bound ($50+$10.00 S&H)
[ ] *Early Manuscripts, Church Fathers, & the Authorized
Version* by Dr. Jack Moorman, $20+$7 S&H. Hardback
[ ] Send *Forever Settled--Bible Documents & History Survey*
by Dr. Jack Moorman, $20+$7 S&H. Hardback book
[ ] Send *When the KJB Departs from the So-Called "Majority
Text"* By Dr. Jack Moorman ($17.00 + $7.00 S&H)

More Books By Dr. Jack Moorman

[ ] Send *Missing in Modern Bibles--Nestle/Aland/NIV Errors*
by Dr. Jack Moorman, $8+$7 S&H
[ ] Send *The Doctrinal Heart of the Bible—Removed from Mod-
ern Versions* by Dr. Jack Moorman, VCR, $15 +$7 S&H
Send or Call Orders to:
THE BIBLE FOR TODAY
900 Park Ave., Collingswood, NJ 08108
Phone: 856-854-4452; FAX:--2464; Orders: 1-800 JOHN 10:9
E-Mail Orders: BFT@BibleForToday.org; Credit Cards OK

Order Blank (p. 5)

Name:_____

Address:_____

City & State:_____Zip:_____

Credit Card #:_____Expires:_____
[ ] Send *Modern Bibles--The Dark Secret* by Dr. Jack Moorman, $5+$4 S&H
[ ] Send *Samuel P. Tregelles--The Man Who Made the Critical Text Acceptable to Bible Believers* by Dr. Moorman ($5+$3)
[ ] Send *8,000 Differences Between TR & CT* by Dr. Jack Moorman [$20 + $7.00 S&H] a hardback book

Books By or About Dean Burgon
[ ] Send *The Revision Revised* by Dean Burgon ($25 + $7 S&H) A hardback book, 640 pages in length
[ ] Send *356 Doctrinal Errors in the NIV & Other Modern Versions*, 100-large-pages, $10.00+$7 S&H
[ ] Send *The Last 12 verses of Mark* by Dean Burgon ($15+$7 S&H) A hardback book 400 pages
[ ] Send *The Traditional Text* hardback by Burgon ($15+$5 S&H) A hardback book, 384 pages in length
[ ] Send *Causes of Corruption* by Burgon ($16+$5 S&H) A hardback book, 360 pages in length

More Books By or About Dean Burgon
[ ] Send *Inspiration and Interpretation*, Dean Burgon ($25+$7 S&H) A hardback book, 610 pages in length
[ ] Send *Burgon's Warnings on Revision* by DAW ($7+$5 S&H) A perfect bound book, 120 pages in length
[ ] Send *Westcott & Hort's Greek Text & Theory Refuted by Burgon's Revision Revised--Summarized* by Dr. D. A. Waite ($7.00+$5 S&H), 120 pages, perfect bound
[ ] Send *Dean Burgon's Confidence in KJB* by DAW ($5+$4)
[ ] Send *Vindicating Mark 16:9-20* by Dr. Waite ($5+$4S&H)
Send or Call Orders to:
THE BIBLE FOR TODAY
900 Park Ave., Collingswood, NJ 08108
Phone: 856-854-4452; FAX:--2464; Orders: 1-800 JOHN 10:9
E-Mail Orders: BFT@BibleForToday.org; Credit Cards OK

Order Blank (p. 6)

Name:_____

Address:_____

City & State:_____Zip:_____

Credit Card #:_____Expires:_____

More Books By or About Dean Burgon
[ ] Send *Summary of Traditional Text* by Dr. Waite ($5 +$4)
[ ] Send *Summary of Causes of Corruption*, DAW ($5+$4)
[ ] Send *Summary of Inspiration* by Dr. Waite ($5+$4 S&H)

More Books by Dr. D. A. Waite
[ ] Send *Making Marriage Melodious* by Pastor D. A. Waite
($7+$5 S&H), perfect bound, 112 pages

Books by D. A. Waite, Jr.
[ ] Send *Readability of A.V. (KJB)* by D. A. Waite, Jr. ($7+$4)
[ ] Send *4,114 Definitions from the Defined King James Bible*
by D. A. Waite, Jr. ($7.00+$5.00 S&H)
[ ] Send *The Doctored New Testament* by D. A. Waite, Jr.
($25+$7.00 S&H) Greek MSS differences shown, hardback
[ ] Send *Defined King James Bible* lg. prt. leather ($40+$10)
[ ] Send *Defined King James Bible* med. leather $35+$8.50)

Miscellaneous Authors
[ ] Send *The Attack on the Canon of Scripture* by Dr. H. D.
Williams, perfect bound ($15.00 + $7.00 S&H)
[ ] Send *Word-For-Word Translating of The Received Texts* by
Dr. H. D. Williams, 288 pages, paperback ($10+$7 S&H).
[ ] Send *Guide to Textual Criticism* by Edward Miller
($11+$7 S&H) a hardback book
[ ] Send *Scrivener's Greek New Testament Underlying the
King James Bible*, hardback, ($14 + $7 S&H)
[ ] Send *Scrivener's Annotated Greek New Testament*, by Dr.
Frederick Scrivener: Hardback--($35+$7 S&H);
Genuine Leather--($45+$7 S&H)

Send or Call Orders to:
THE BIBLE FOR TODAY
900 Park Ave., Collingswood, NJ 08108
Phone: 856-854-4452; FAX:--2464; Orders: 1-800 JOHN 10:9
E-Mail Orders: BFT@BibleForToday.org; Credit Cards OK

Order Blank (p. 7)

Name:_____

Address:_____

City & State:_____Zip:_____

Credit Card #:_____Expires:_____

Miscellaneous Authors (Continued)

[ ] Send *Why Not the King James Bible?--An Answer to James White's KJVO Book* by Dr. K. D. DiVietro, $10+$7 S&H

[ ] Send Brochure #1: "Over *1000 Titles Defending the KJB/TR*" Compiled by Dr. D. A. Waite. No Charge

Send or Call Orders to:
THE BIBLE FOR TODAY
900 Park Ave., Collingswood, NJ 08108
Phone: 856-854-4452; FAX:--2464; Orders: 1-800 JOHN 10:9
E-Mail Orders: BFT@BibleForToday.org; Credit Cards OK

Pastor D. A. Waite, Th.D., Ph.D.
200 More Questions

- **The Reason For This Book.** I have put into print both The First, Second, Third, Fourth, and Fifth 200 Questions and Answers (BFT #3309, #3473, #3482, #3494, & #4014), but I still have more questions that have been asked me through the years. This book takes up questions ##1001 to 1200. Some of these might be your questions as well.

- **The Goal of This Book.** The goal of this Sixth 200 Questions and Answers is similar to that of the First, Second, Third, Fourth, and Fifth 200 Questions. I want to give our readers an understanding of where I stand on many additional controversial issues.

- **The Name of This Book.** The title of the book, The Sixth 200 Questions Answered by Dr. D. A. Waite, bears witness to the fact that there was a First , Second, Third, Fourth & Fifth 200 Questions. It implied that there could one day be a Sixth 200 Questions. This has come to pass now.

- **The Usefulness of This Book.** The author of a book can never predict whether or not his book is either useful or not useful. This depends on the opinions and needs of the readers. Are they fully informed on the topics that are discussed? Do they know the answers? If they do not know the answers, do they really want to find them out? It seems that many people are not concerned with Biblical subjects. The tool that makes this book useful to those who read it is the lengthy Index of Words and Phrases. You will find this Index very helpful to you.

www.BibleForToday.org

BFT 4058 BK   **ISBN #978-1-56848-087-9**

www.ingramcontent.com/pod-product-compliance
Lightning Source LLC
Chambersburg PA
CBHW071433090426
42737CB00011B/1644